ZHENG HE'S VOYAGES TO THE WESTERN OCEANS

郑和下西洋

王介南 著

Tranlated by Ego

五洲传播出版社

China Intercontinental Press

图书在版编目（CIP）数据

郑和下西洋：汉英对照／王介南著；译谷译.—北京：五洲传播出版社，2010.1

ISBN 978-7-5085-1702-5

Ⅰ．①郑…　Ⅱ．①王…②译…　Ⅲ．①郑和下西洋－汉、英　Ⅳ．①K248.105

中国版本图书馆CIP数据核字（2009）第192503号

中外文化交流故事丛书（Roads to the World）

顾　　问：赵启正　沈锡麟　潘　岳
　　　　　周黎明（美）李　莎（加）威廉·林赛（英）
主　　编：荆孝敏　邓锦辉
著　　者：王介南
翻　　译：Ego
责任编辑：高　磊
设计指导：田　林
封面绘画：李　骐
设计制作：北京原色印象文化艺术中心
图　　片：范春歌　王介南　郑黎明　郑　明　CFP　《经典杂志》等

郑和下西洋

Zheng He's Voyages to the Western Oceans

出版发行　五洲传播出版社（北京市海淀区北小马厂6号　邮编：100038）
电　　话　8610-58891281（发行部）
网　　址　www.cicc.org.cn
承 印 者　北京外文印务有限公司
版　　次　2010年1月第1版第1次印刷
开　　本　720×965毫米　1/16
印　　张　10.25
定　　价　78.00元

Contents 目 录

FOREWORD

It has been a long and exciting history of tremendous cultural exchange between China and other countries. In terms of culture, economy, ideology, and personnel, these exchanges between China and other countries can be dated back to the times of Qin and Han dynasties—directly or indirectly, by land or sea. The long-term and multi-faceted cultural exchange helps the world to understand more about China and the rest of the world, enriching the common wealth of mankind—both materially and spiritually.

The book series entitled *Roads to the World* offers the most splendid stories in the entire history of Sino-foreign cultural exchange. We hereby offer them to foreign students learning the Chinese language, and to foreign readers who have a keen interest in Chinese culture. These stories depict important personalities, events, and phenomena in various fields of cultural exchange between China and other nations, and among different peoples. By reading the books, you may understand China and Chinese civilization profoundly, and the close link between Chinese civilization and other civilizations of the world. The books highlight the efforts and contributions of Chinese people and Chinese civilization in the world's cultural interchange. They reflect mankind's common spiritual pursuit and the orientation of values.

This book tells the story of Zheng He's seven voyages to the western oceans. Zheng He is a Chinese navigator of the Ming Dynasty, who led a massive fleet and visited more than 30 countries and regions on the coast of the West Pacific and the Indian Ocean from 1405 to 1433, half a century prior to the inception of the Great Era of Navigation in Europe. His voyages strengthened the friendly relations between China and the Southeast Asia, South Asia, West Asia, and East African nations in the Ming Dynasty, and conducted unprecedented economic and cultural exchanges, achieving a host of win-win results.

前　言

　　中国与其他国家、民族之间的文化交流具有悠久而曲折的历史。在中国与外国之间，通过间接的和直接的、陆路的和海路的、有形的和无形的多种渠道，各种文化、经济、思想、人员方面的交流，可以上溯至秦汉时代，下及于当今社会。长期的、多方面的交流，增进了中国与其他国家、民族之间的了解，使人类的共同财富（物质的和精神的）更加丰富。

　　中外文化交流故事丛书（Roads to the World）的宗旨，是从中外文化交流的历史长河中，选择那些最璀璨的明珠，通过讲故事的方式，介绍给学习汉语的外国学生和对中国文化感兴趣的外国读者。这些故事描述中国与其他国家、民族在各个领域文化交流中的重要人物、事件和现象，以使外国读者能够更深入地理解中国，理解中国文明，理解中国文明与其他各文明之间的密切关系，以及中国人和中国文明在这种交流过程中所作出的努力和贡献，并尽力彰显人类共同的精神追求与价值取向。

　　本书讲述的是中国明代航海家郑和率领船队七次下西洋的故事。1405—1433年，在欧洲大航海时代到来的半个多世纪之前，郑和先后七次率领庞大的船队访问了西太平洋和印度洋沿岸的30多个国家和地区，加深了明代中国与东南亚、南亚、西亚、东非地区国家之间的友好关系，开展了规模空前的经济文化交流，取得了双赢的效果。

I

Sanbao Eunuch Zheng He

Zheng He (1371–1433) was an outstanding politician and world-renowned navigator. With an aim to establish and develop the friendly ties and economic and cultural exchange between China and overseas countries, Zheng He led 100 vessels and more than 27,000 officials and soldiers to visit more than 30 countries and regions in Southeast Asia, South Asia, West Asia and East Africa through seven trip in a period of 28 years between 1405 to 1433 under the orders of Emperor Yongle during the Ming Dynasty (Yongle was on the throne from 1403–1424). The fleet departed from Nanjing, the capital of the Ming Dynasty. It launched from the Liujiagang Port in Suzhou, sailed past the South China Sea, the Strait of Malacca, the Indian Ocean, the Persian Gulf, the Red Sea and reached coasts in East Africa. All told, it navigated 160,000 sea miles. It established peaceful and friendly relationships with the countries and regions visited, carried out economic and cultural exchanges and received warm welcomes and hospitality

1

三宝太监郑和

郑和（1371—1433）是中国历史上杰出的外交家和世界历史上名闻遐迩的航海家。为了恢复和发展中国与海外诸国的友好关系和经济文化往来，他奉明朝永乐皇帝（1403—1424年在位）之命，从1405年至1433年的28年间，连续七次出访西洋。他从明朝京师南京启程，在苏州刘家港整队出航，云帆高张，昼夜星驰，际天而行，过南海，穿马六甲海峡，渡印度洋，经波斯湾，达红海，到东非海岸。航程总计16万海里，遍访东南亚、南亚、西亚和东非30多个国家和地区，与所访国家和地区建立和平友好关系，开展经济文化交流，

from people in more than 30 countries in Southeast Asia, South Asia, West Asia and East Africa. Zheng He's voyages to the western oceans were a miracle in the history of navigation the huge ships involved, the massive number of sailors, the sheer scale, long distances and time spent at sea. The voyages are also a splendid chapter in the peaceful diplomatic activities of ancient China for the deep and friendly ties established, broad economic and trade exchanges and prosperous cultural blends it accomplished. Zheng He defeated risks associated with sailing in his era with exquisite navigation skills. He is regarded as one of the 30 most influential explorers of the past 1,000 years.

The goals of Zheng He's voyages to the western oceans were opening, exchange and development—including the development of Chinese and foreign politics, economy and culture via opening and exchanges. Zheng He's voyages to the western oceans brought mutual benefits to Ming Dynasty China and Asian and African countries, enhanced bilateral friendships, developed Sino–foreign ocean shipping and international trade, promoted the prosperity of the Silk Road at Sea and resulted in Chinese and foreign exchanges of unprecedented scale.

Zheng He's voyages to the western oceans were a splendid chapter not only in history of marine navigation in China but also the world. They have been confirmed and warmly praised by Chinese people. In his *Biography of the Grand Navigator Zheng He*, Liang Qichao (1873–1929),

受到亚非国家人民的热烈欢迎和盛情款待。郑和的航海活动，以船舶之巨、船员之众、规模之大、航程之长、历时之久，创造了世界航海史上的奇迹；以友好交往之深、经贸往来之广、文化交融之盛，造就了中国古代和平外交的辉煌。郑和以其精湛的航海技术战胜了帆船时代的海上风险，被誉为"过去1000年间最具历史影响的30位世界探险家之一"。

郑和下西洋这一盛举的本质是开放、交流和发展；发展中外政治、经济和文化是目的，开放与交流是手段。郑和下西洋取得了明代中国与亚非国家双赢的效果，在政治外交方面增进了双边的传统友谊，经济方面发展了中外远洋国际贸易，促进了海上丝绸之路的繁荣，文化方面展开了空前规模的中外文化交流。

郑和下西洋不但在中国航海史上写下了光辉的一页，而且在世界航海史上谱写了灿烂的篇章，因而受到中国人民的充分肯定和热情赞颂。近代中国启蒙思想家梁启超（1873—1929）在《祖国大航海家郑和传》中说："反观郑君，则全世界历史上所号称航海伟人，能与比肩者，何其寡也。"中国民主革命先行者孙中山先生（1866—1925）在《建国方略》

an enlightenment ideologist in modern China wrote: "Only few number of grand navigators in the history of the world can match Zheng He." Sun Yat-sen (1866–1925), the driver of the Chinese democratic revolution, praised Zheng He's voyages to the western oceans highly as "a miracle in the history and future of China" in his book *The International Development of China*. Zheng He's voyages to the western oceans also received high praise and a great deal of attention from scholars of all countries. J.J.L.Duyrendak (1889–1954) in the Netherlands described the voyages as "great sea trips of the Chinese people in early 15th century." Joseph Needham (1900–1995) from the U.K. praised the voyages as the greatest navigation ventures in Chinese history. Terada Takanobu (1931–   ) from Japan says: "the voyages completed by Zheng He were really a great undertaking. They were not only the biggest offshore activity in the history of China, but also the largest one among similar undertakings completed by human beings till early 15th century. The voyages started in the so–called Great Era of Navigation dozens of years later paled by comparison with Zheng He's voyages to the western oceans." Zheng He's voyages to the western oceans started in 1405, 87 years earlier than Christopher Columbus' (1451–1506) arrival in America in 1492, 83 years earlier than Bartholomeu Dias' (1455–1500) crossing the Cape of Good Hope in 1488, 92 years earlier than Vasco da Gama's (1469–1524) arrival in Calicut, India, in 1497, and 114 years before Ferdinand Magellan (1480–1521)

中，赞扬郑和下西洋"为中国超前轶后之奇举"。
与此同时，郑和下西洋也受到各国学者的高度重视和
盛情赞扬。荷兰的戴文达（J.J.L.Duyrendak，1889—
1954）说它是"15世纪初中国人伟大的海上航行"。
英国的李约瑟（Joseph Needham，1900—1995）称赞
它"是中国历史上最伟大的航海探险"。日本的寺田
隆信（1931— ）则说："郑和完成的航海事业，应
该说的确是伟大的事业。这不仅是中国历史上最大
的海上活动，而且是直至15世纪初，在人类所进行的
同样事业中规模最大的一次。在它的面前，迟于数
十年才开始的所谓的'大航海时代'的种种航海，便
相形见绌了。"郑和下西洋开始于1405年，比哥伦
布（Cyistopher Columbus，1451—1506）1492年到达
美洲早87年，比迪亚士（Bartholomeu Dias，1455—
1500）1488年发现好望角早83年，比达·伽马（Vasco
da Gama，1469—1524）1497年到达印度卡利卡特早
92年，比麦哲伦（Ferdinand Magellan，1480—1521）
1519年开始环球航行早114年。不仅如此，郑和的船队
在西太平洋、印度洋上建立的亚非海上交通贸易网，
还为其后欧洲人的东来和欧洲人的环球航行创造了条

undertook his voyage around the world in 1519. Moreover, the Asia-Africa offshore traffic and trade network Zheng He's fleet established in the Western Pacific Ocean and Indian Ocean created conditions for Europeans coming from the east and navigation around the world. It can be said that Zheng He's voyage to the western oceans was the forerunner of the great geographical discoveries that made active contributions to the Great Era of Navigation and created direct links between east and west.

Zheng He's original surname was Ma. He took the first name He and styled a Sanbao. He was born in 1371, during the Ming Dynasty, into a family of the Hui nationality, which traditionally follows Islam, in Hedai Village, Baoshan Township, Kunyang Prefecture (today's Jinning County, Kunming City), Yunnan Province of China. His sixth generation ancestor Sayyid Ajjal Shams al-Din Omar (1211–1279) was stationed in Xianyang and won merit when following Mongolian noble Genghis Khan in war. During the reign of Kublai Khan, in the Yuan Dynasty, Sayyid Ajjal Shams al-Din Omar assumed the post of Pingzhang Zhengshi or governor of Yunnan Province. In his six-year tenure, Omar made outstanding political achievements and was loved and respected by the people. After his death, he was awarded the title of "Xianyang King." His offspring lived in Yunnan and inherited the title of Dianyanghou. The family lived side by side with the Han people for generations and, over time, began following the customs of Han, including

件。因之可以说，郑和下西洋是"地理大发现"的先导，它为"大航海时代"的到来作出了积极的贡献，也为地球的东西两方联成一体作出了直接的贡献。

郑和，本姓马，名和，字三宝，公元1371年生于明代中国云南省昆阳州（今昆明市晋宁县）宝山乡和代村一个世代信奉伊斯兰教的回族家庭。他的六世祖赛典赤·瞻思丁（Sayyid Ajjal Shams al-Din Omar，1211—1279）因随蒙古贵族首领成吉思汗征战有功驻镇咸阳；元世祖忽必烈即位后，赛典赤·瞻思丁出任

云南晋宁郑和故居
Former residence of Zheng He in Jinning, Yunnan Province

adopting the surname Ma. Zheng He's grandfather and father all visited Tianfang, a holy land of Islam (known as Mecca in Saudi Arabia today) to make a pilgrimage. They were given the honorable title of "Hazhi". Zheng He's father was named Ma Hazhi. He was tall and of a sturdy stature. He was upright and willing to help others and was well respected.

When he was young, Zheng He was clever and handsome with a high forehead and big eyes. He was loved by his neighbors. He grew up and learnt from his parents the stories of his grandfather's visit to Mecca despite the distance and hardship of the sea route. These stories inspired his desire to travel to the holy land of Mecca and his curiosity to explore overseas countries. Zheng He's parents guided him to study the Arabic language and Islamic sutras and paid close attentions to his physical body and the cultivation of his courage and perseverance.

In 1382, when Zheng He was 12 years old, armies of the Ming Dynasty occupied Yunnan. Zheng He's father died in the war. Zheng He was captured by Ming armies. They took him to Nanjing and castrated him into a young eunuch. The Hongwu Emperor Zhu Yuanzhang (on the throne from 1368–1398) gave Zheng He to his fourth son Prince Yan Zhu Di (guarded in Beijing) as a young domestic servant. As a young domestic servant, Zheng He had to shoulder a heavy daily workload at the Mansion of Prince Yan, from cleaning up the four treasures of the

云南省平章政事（相当于今省长），在任六年，政绩显著，深受人们爱戴，死后封为"咸阳王"。其子孙世居云南，袭封滇阳侯。由于长时间与汉族共处，改从汉俗，定姓马。

郑和的祖父和父亲都曾不远万里朝觐伊斯兰教圣地天方（今沙特阿拉伯麦加），故被荣称"哈只"。郑和父亲马哈只，身材高大，为人正直，乐于助人，深得当地百姓的尊敬。

郑和幼时容貌俊秀，聪明伶俐，甚得乡邻们的喜爱。稍稍懂事以后，常从父母口中听到祖辈不畏海路艰辛，战风斗浪，长途跋涉朝觐麦加的生动故事，使他幼小的心灵萌发了对远方圣地麦加的向往，产生出探索海外异域的好奇心。郑和的父母引导他认真学习阿拉伯语言文字和伊斯兰教经典，并注重他的体魄锻炼和勇气、毅力的培养。

1382年郑和12岁时，明朝军队攻占云南。战乱中，他父亲不幸身亡，他为明军所俘，被带回京师南京后遭阉割，成为一名小太监。洪武皇帝朱元璋(1368—1398年在位)将他赐给第四个儿子、镇守北京的燕王朱棣做家奴。

study (writing brush, ink stick, ink slab and paper) and ancient books to cleaning the rooms and looking after Prince Yan. Zheng He worked quickly and diligently and did everything properly. When he noticed others did not have time to do something, he always offered to lend a helping hand. As a result, Zheng He was praised by everyone in the Mansion of Prince Yan. However, Zheng He had always had great aspirations and never forgot his childhood longing to travel. Every day, after finishing his heavy workload, he got up early and slept late to study regardless of how tired he was. The Mansion of Prince Yan had a classroom and the prince hired well-learnt officials to act as teachers to teach the children of people who worked in the mansion. Noticing that Zheng He was curious and ambitious, Prince Yan Zhu Di arranged for him to study in the classroom. Zheng He studied carefully and assiduously. In only a few years, he learnt much and grew to become a full-bodied and handsome man. Around that time, someone described Zheng He as "7-chi-high, 10-wei of waist, with a high forehead and small nose, clear eyebrows and eyes, white ears, shell-like teeth, tiger-style actions, a bell-like voice, alert, wise and aware of war." Wise and capable as he was, he did things carefully and had great ambitions. Gradually, Prince Yan began to appreciate him. In four years of the civil war for the Ming Dynasty crown, Zheng He helped Prince Yan Zhu Di fight from south to north and distinguished himself. In 1402, Prince Yan Zhu Di became emperor (Emperor

作为一名小家奴，郑和在燕王府邸每天承担的劳役是相当繁重的，从整理文房四宝、古文典籍到洒扫内室、侍奉燕王起居，粗活细差样样都干。他干事麻利，手脚勤快，一件件办得妥妥帖帖；见到其他奴仆干不完的事，他便主动上前相助，所以博得燕王府中上上下下的称赞。少有大志的郑和，并没有忘记幼年的憧憬，他每天拖着劳累下来的疲惫身躯，起早摸黑地发奋自学读书。

燕王府里设有书堂，聘请有学问的官员充任教师，教育府里做事人的子女。燕王朱棣见郑和好学上进，便安排他进书堂读书。郑和读书认真、刻苦，不几年就懂得了许多知识。其身体也出落得体格魁梧，相貌俊朗。当时有人描述他"身高七尺，腰大十围，四岳（指额）峻而鼻小，眉目分明，耳白过面，齿如编贝，行如虎步，声如宏钟，博辩机敏，长于智略，知兵习战"。他因为精明能干、做事认真，且有志向，渐为燕王朱棣赏识。在争夺明朝皇位的内战中，郑和助燕王朱棣南北征战，建有奇功。1402年燕王朱棣称帝（即明成祖，明朝第三位皇帝，年号永乐，1403年为永乐元年）后不久，即于1404年春节，因他

Ming Chengzu, the third emperor of the Ming Dynasty and took the name of Yongle and 1403 was the first year of Yongle's reign). Shortly after that, in the Spring Festival of 1404, Zheng He was given the surname Zheng for his accomplishments fighting at Zhengcunba, Tongxian County, Hebei. He was promoted to Neiguanjian Eunuch, becoming the leader of Neiguanjian. Neiguanjian was responsible for the construction of palaces and tombs, arrangements at weddings and funeral ceremonies of royalty, procurement of utensils used in the palace and rare treasures. Zheng He became a trusted subordinate and a useful assistant of Emperor Yongle.

Zheng He was a devout of Ismal and also a disciple of the Buddha initiated into monkhood (his religious name was Fushan or Fujixiang). In Buddhism, Buddha, Dharma and Sangha are regarded as Sanbao. The term Buddha refers to Sakyamuni, the founder of Buddhism, but also generally to all people with a deep understanding of Buddhism. Dharma refers to the doctrines of Buddhism and generally refers to all Confucian classics or religious scriptures in Buddhism. The term sangha refers to monks who sincerely believe in and promote Buddhism Doctrines and generally refers to all devout disciples. In the viewpoint of Buddhism, all disciples who believe in Buddhism should come over and adhere to Sanbao. Zheng He's name of "Sanbao Eunuch" used by people is closely linked to his devotion to Buddhism. There was another well known story. Zheng He had an elder brother

在河北通县郑村坝作战有功而赐姓郑，并擢升为"内官监太监"，成为内官监的首领。内官监负责营建宫殿陵墓、安排皇室婚丧礼仪、采办宫廷陈设的器物和奇珍异宝等事务。此时的郑和已成为永乐皇帝倚重的心腹和得力助手。

郑和既是虔诚的伊斯兰教徒，又是受了菩萨戒的佛家弟子。佛教奉佛、法、僧为"三宝"。"佛"，指佛教创始人释迦牟尼，也泛指佛门中一切大知大觉的人；"法"，指佛教的教义，也泛指佛门中一切经

郑和故乡——云南晋宁县三宝楼
Hometown of Zheng He – Sanbao Building in Jinning County, Yunnan Province

and an elder sister. He was the third child in his family and was nicknamed Sanbao (referring to the third son). He was therefore called "Sanbao Eunuch." According to historical data, Emperor Xuande of the Ming Dynasty Zhu Zhanji (in the throne from 1425–1435) gave Zheng He the title of Sanbao Eunuch in 1431 for having served three emperors—Yongle, Hongxi and Xuande, and loyally assisted Chengzu, Renzong and Xuanzong emperors. As Zheng He's outstanding achievements spread, the title Sanbao Eunuch became associated with Zheng He. As a person who respected Buddhism and Islam, he found it suitable to visit Asian and African countries which take Buddhism and Islam as the national religion. The common faith and the sentimental ties that connect people in Asian and African countries were helpful to establish friendly relationships and alleviate intense situations between all countries. Zheng He was educated at the Mansion of Prince Yan and showcased his outstanding talents in military command. These features, in addition to his eloquence and resourcefulness, made him a brilliant diplomatic and military leader. These conditions allowed Zheng He to act as an envoy and complete the political and diplomatic obligations assigned by Emperor Yongle of going to far western oceans.

书典籍；"僧"，指笃信和宣扬佛教教义的僧侣，也泛指一切虔诚的信徒。按佛门观点，凡崇信佛教者，都要归顺、依附这"三宝"。郑和被世人称为"三宝太监"，当与他皈依佛门有很大关系。另有一种说法：郑和有一兄一姐，他排行第三，小名三宝，故人称"三宝太监"。另据史料记载，1431年明宣宗朱瞻基（1425—1435年在位）因郑和历经永乐、洪熙、宣德三朝，忠心辅佐成祖、仁宗、宣宗，而赐封郑和为三保太监。由于郑和业绩广为流传，久而久之，"三保（或三宝）太监"就成为郑和专有的代名词。崇奉佛教、伊斯兰教这两种宗教的人，很适合访问以佛教、伊斯兰教为国教的亚非国家。因为共同的宗教信仰，乃是维系亚非各国人民的感情纽带，它有助于沟通和建立相互间的友好关系，缓解各国之间的紧张局势。郑和在燕王府里受过良好的文化教育，在征战中又显露出卓越的军事指挥才能，且富有口才，足智多谋，具有外交家和军事统帅的潜质，这就为郑和担任正使完成永乐皇帝交付的下西洋这一重大政治外交使命准备了条件。

II

Seven voyages to western oceans

In 1405, the 34-year-old Zheng He confidently accepted an order from Emperor Yongle and started the arduous task of traveling to western oceans with a fleet as chief imperial envoy.

Under his leadership, the fleet was active in Southeast Asia, South Asia and East Africa. According to Zheng He's strategy, the fleet navigated westward step by step in a ladder shape in line with a "three-layered" structure—taking Southeast Asia as the base, the Indian South Peninsula and coastal countries as the center, and navigating to West Asia and East Africa. With an aim to establish a solid base in Southeast Asia, Zheng He's first, second and third voyages focused on Southeast Asia, and the end goal was reaching Guli in South Asia. In the fourth and fifth voyages, the end point was moved westward to Hormuz in West Asia. In the sixth and seventh voyages, the destination was pushed to Malindi, Kenya in East Africa. Zheng He, with his excellent command ability and

2

七下西洋

1405年，时年34岁的郑和满怀信心地领受永乐皇帝的敕谕，以下西洋正使、钦差总兵的身份，开始了统领船队下西洋的艰巨任务。

郑和统领的船队主要活动在东南亚、南亚和东非

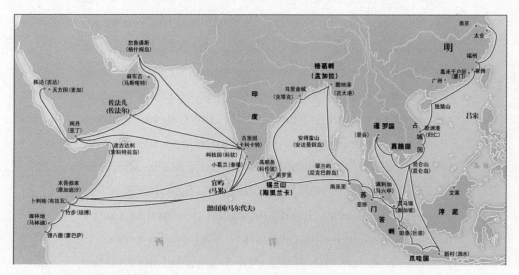

郑和下西洋航线图

Navigation map for Zheng He's voyages to the western oceans

outstanding diplomatic and military wisdom, successfully organized and accomplished these difficult ocean voyages.

First voyage to the west oceans (1405–1407)

On July 11, 1405, Zheng He started his first voyage to the west oceans. Shortly after, he led the fleet out of Nanjing, the capital of the dynasty, and into the Yangtze River. He stopped at Liujiagang Port in Suzhou at the entrance of the Yangtze River to wait for further orders.

That late autumn, a solemn ceremony to launch the trip was held at Liujiagang Port to send off Zheng He, the envoy of Ming Dynasty. The fleet of 62 vessels then navigated from the East Sea to the South China Sea under Zheng He's leadership.

After arriving at Taiping Port, Changle County in Fujian Province, the fleet berthed at the port to wait for the northeast monsoon. While waiting, Zheng He and his officers and soldiers held a solemn ceremony to offer sacrifices to the god of navigation—the Celestial Queen —to seek for protection. After the monsoon passed, the fleet sailed off from Wuhumen (currently at the Minjiang River Estuary), entered the South China Sea after passing through the Taiwan Strait and sailed downwind for 10 days to Zhancheng (south part of Vietnam at present). After a short rest, the fleet sailed downwind for 20 days to Java. At that time, Java was governed by east and

三大区域。郑和经略这三大区域，在总体战略上是按"三级"式格局，呈梯状层层西进的，即以东南亚为后方基地，以印度南半岛及沿海诸国为经略中心，远届西亚、东非。为了建立稳固的东南亚后方基地，郑和将第一、第二、第三次远航的重心放在东南亚，远航终点为南亚的古里；第四、第五两次，向西推进至西亚的忽鲁谟斯（霍尔木兹）；第六、第七两次推进至东非肯尼亚的麻林（马林迪）。郑和以他卓越的指挥才能和杰出的外交、军事智略，出色地组织并完成了七次远航的重大任务。

第一次下西洋（1405—1407）

1405年7月11日，郑和奉旨第一次下西洋。不久，他指挥下西洋船队陆续从京师南京下关开船，浩浩荡荡进入长江，驶抵长江口的苏州刘家港集结待命。

同年深秋，刘家港举行隆重的开航仪式，欢送出使西洋各国的明朝使者郑和启航。然后，62艘海船组成的长长船队，在郑和的率领下，浩浩荡荡地航行在东海的海面，向南海驶去。

在茫茫东海中破浪前进的郑和船队到福建长乐县

west kings. Upon the arrival of Zheng He's fleet, the two kings were fighting a war. Seeing Zheng He's fleet, the winner west king mistakenly thought the east kind was receiving reinforcements and killed more than 170 people. When the truth came out, the west king felt great fear and dispatched an envoy to apologize. Considering the west king of Java to be the offender and the entire case a misapprehension, Emperor Yongle criticized the king and ordered him to pay compensation of 60,000 *liang* (taels) to settle the matter.

Zheng He's fleet left Java and sailed downwind for eight days to Jiugang. From there it sailed downwind for eight more days to Manlajia.

Manlajia (today's Malacca), was a country in the Malaysian peninsula in early 15th century. Manlajia controlled the Strait of Malacca, the traffic hub between the Pacific Ocean and the Indian Ocean, a required route for vessel. In early 15th century, the Ming Dynasty and Manlajia exchanged frequent visits. After ascending to the throne, Emperor Yongle dispatched Yin Qing to visit Manlajia. Upon the arrival of Zheng He's fleet, the king of Manlajia led his officials to welcome Zheng He at the port in magnificent dresses and with an honor guard. Zheng He produced the letter of reference from the Chinese Emperor Yongle to the king of Manlajia and gave him gifts such as double silver seals and garments.

江苏太仓，浏河注入长江处。郑和七次下西洋，船队都是在这里集结后出发。
Taicang, Jiangsu, from which, the Liuhe River enters into the Yangtze River. In Zheng He's seven voyages to the western oceans, the fleet set off from Taicang.

太平港后，驻泊等候东北季风。等候期间，郑和亲率船队官兵隆重祭祀航海保护神——天妃，以求保护。季风来后，再由五虎门（今闽江口）扬帆开航，穿越台湾海峡进入南海，顺风航行十昼夜到达占城国（今越南南部）。在那里作短暂停留后，又顺风航行20昼夜到达爪哇。爪哇有东、西二王。当郑和船队航行至此时，正值东、西二王交战。郑和船队到达时，战胜者西王以为是东王请来的救兵，便一哄而上，乱杀一气，误杀船队队员170余人。真相大白后，西王胆战心惊，立即遣使谢罪。永乐皇帝念其初犯，且为误伤，一番责备之后，令其赔偿黄金6万两了断此事。

　　郑和船队离开爪哇，继续航行，顺风八昼夜到旧

The king of Manlajia extended great thanks to the Chinese envoys and encouraged Zheng He's endeavor. The king not only provided material support to Zheng He but also allowed Zheng He to set up a warehouse in Manlajia to store cargo.

The warehouse was large and made up of an inner part and an outer part. It had a door on each of four sides. In the warehouse, Zheng He stored grain, money and materials to exchange or give away in other countries. Surrounding the warehouse, there were four-door drum towers. The warehouse was both a warehouse and a cargo transshipment station for Zheng He's voyages to the western oceans. The fleet was dispatched to surrounding countries for visits or trade activities after arriving at the warehouse. The vessels returned from these trips and gathered at the warehouse to clear and package cargo, waited for the southwest monsoon in mid May and then sailed back to China. The establishment of such a cargo transshipment station in Manlajia played an important role in Zheng He's expeditions and reflected the profound friendship between China and Manlajia. During Zheng He's voyages to western oceans, Manlajia dispatched envoys to visit China 26 times and each was warmly received by the Ming Dynasty.

After staying in Manlajia for a period of time, Zheng He's fleet sailed westward to the Indian Ocean after

马六甲三宝山一角。三宝山是海外华人的最大坟山，也是华人先贤开拓南洋的见证。
A scene of Mt. Sanbao in Malacca,Malaysia. Mt. Sanbao is the biggest hill cemetery of overseas Chinese, and also the testimony for expansion of Chinese ancestors in Nanyang.

港，又顺风八昼夜到满剌加。

满剌加（今马六甲）是15世纪初在马来半岛兴起的一个国家。它控制着马六甲海峡，这里是太平洋与印度洋之间的交通咽喉，是过往船只的必经之地。15世纪初，中国明朝与满剌加往来不绝，永乐皇帝登基后曾派尹庆到满剌加访问。这次郑和船队一到满剌加，国王便亲率大臣，穿着华丽的盛装，带着仪仗队，前往港口迎接。郑和向国王宣读了中国永乐皇帝的国书，赠送了双台银印、服饰等优厚的礼物。

满剌加国王十分感谢中国使者，大力支持郑和的远航，不仅提供物质援助，还同意郑和在那里建立仓库存放货物。这座仓库规模很大，分为内城和外城两

crossing the Strait of Malacca. The fleet passed Sri Lanka, sailed westward to visit Xiaogelan (today's Quilon in India) and Cochin (today's Cochin at the southwest bank of the Indian Ocean) in the Indian Peninsula and eventually arrived in Guli, the final destination of the voyage.

Guli was located in today's Kerala, India. It is now called Kozhikode. It is a renowned ancient ports in the Indian Ocean. Guli teemed with spices and peppers. The king of Guli believed in Buddhism and there were Muslims in the country. After arriving in Guli, Zheng He handed the letter of credence from Emperor Yongle to Shamidi, king of Guli, gave many gifts to the king and ministers and traded with local businessmen. In the trading process, Zheng He and seamen of the fleet followed local customs, fixed the price by clapping their hands and delivered the cargo the next day. Besides barter, gold, silver and copper cashes were also used to trade.

Guli teemed with wheat and grains. People there were unsophisticated. They gave way to others voluntarily and nobody picked up or pocketed anything lost by someone else. The people of Guli followed Buddhism and respected the cow and elephant. Cow breeders could only drink the milk of the cow but not eat its meat. People who killed cows randomly were punished. Upon learning this, Zheng He ordered his subordinates to respect the local custom.

部分，四周有四个门。仓库里堆放着粮食、金钱以及准备交换和赠送各国的物资。它既是一座仓库，也是郑和下西洋途中的一个货物转运站。下西洋的船队到达这里后，再派到附近一些国家去访问或贸易。去各国访问贸易归来的船只也都到这里集合，整理货物，分类包装，等候五月中旬的西南季风，然后整队返航回国。这样一个货物转运站在满剌加的建立，对郑和航海任务的完成起了很大的作用，它体现了中国满剌加两国间的深厚友谊。郑和下西洋期间，满剌加26次遣使来中国，每次都受到明政府的盛情接待。

郑和船队在满剌加逗留一段时间后，又西行穿过马六甲海峡，进入印度洋，过锡兰，西行访问印度半岛的小葛兰(今印度奎隆)、柯枝（今印度西南岸科钦，Cochin），最后到达终点站古里。

古里位于今印度喀拉拉邦，现名卡利卡特(Calicut)，为印度著名的古港之一。古里国盛产香料胡椒。古里国王崇信佛教，但国内亦有伊斯兰教徒。郑和到达古里后，向国王沙米地递交永乐皇帝的国书，赠送国王和大臣许多礼品，随后与当地商人进行贸易。贸易时，郑和船队队员遵守当地风俗：击掌定

At the end of the visit, the king of Guli entrusted Zheng He to bring a belt made from 50 *liang* (taels) of gold and enchased with various treasures to Emperor Yongle of the Ming Dynasty as a gift to express his affection towards the friendly country of China. Zheng He extended thanks for the hospitality of the king of Guli and set up a stone monument with an inscription: "Although Guli is more than 100,000 li to China, its people and custom are similar with those of China. The stele is set up here to tell the next generations." This was the first stele Zheng He set up in an overseas country and evidence of the friendly ties between China and Guli. In each one of his seven voyages, Zheng He passed through Guli and Guli dispatched regular envoys to China.

In the return voyage, Zheng He led the fleet to visit Jiugang. Jiugang was also called Jugang (now Palembang, Indonesia) and was called Sanfoqi State in Ming Dynasty, which was situated to the northeast of Sumatra Island. During the early Ming Dynasty, many Chinese went south to Sanfoqi. Among them was Liang Daoming, born in Nanhai, Guangdong Province. Later, thousands of people in Fujian and Guangdong provinces went to him and elected him as their leader. Another ringleader of Sanfoqi was Chen Zuyi, who had been a local tyrant in Chaozhou, Guangdong Province. Later, he became one of the headmen of Sanfoqi. Chen Zuyi became a pirate,

郑和到访印度古里（想象图）
Zheng He's visit to Culicut, India (imagination)

价，择日交货，不得反悔。在交易中，除了以物换物外，还使用金、银、铜钱。

古里国盛产麦谷，民风淳朴，行者让路，道不拾遗，信奉佛教，尊敬牛和象，养牛只准喝其奶，不准杀吃其肉，私自杀牛者要被处罚。郑和了解到这些情况，命令部下尊重当地风俗。

郑和结束访问时，古里国王将该国工匠用50两赤金抽丝编织并镶有各种珍宝的一条宝带，作为礼物委托郑和赠给永乐皇帝，以表达对友邦中国的情谊。郑和感谢古里国王的盛情，并立碑石纪念。碑文说："其国去中国十万余里，民物咸若，熙同风，刻石于兹，永示万世。"这是郑和在海外所立的最早的一块

often taking groups of bandits to rob passing vessels and businessmen. In 1407, Chen Zuyi learnt that Zheng He's fleet would come to Jiugang with many treasures. He quietly planned a robbery.

Another patriotic overseas Chinese named Shi Jinqing, who was born in Guangdong Province, hated Chen Zuyi's acts of piracy. When Zheng He's fleet arrived at Jiugang, he immediately reported Chen Zuyi's plots to Zheng He. At first, Zheng He tried to persuade Chen Zuyi to give up evil and return to good. He announced his status as an imperial envoy and prepared for defense. Although Chen Zuyi was friendly to Zheng He's face, he still thought of a

Nanyang

Nanyang was the name of Southeast Asia region in the Ming and Qing dynasties, and was based on a concept with China as its center. Nanyang includes the Malay Archipelago, the Philippines, the Indonesia Archipelago as well as the coastal areas of Indo-China Peninsula and the Malay Peninsula. In the Ming Dynasty and after the dying out of Ming Dynasty, migrants of Han Nationality flocked to the region for living and permanent residence, which was known as "going to Nanyang".

Nanyang was a comparative concept with Xiyang, Dongyang and Beiyang. Xiyang refers to the Indian Ocean region to the west of the Malacca Strait as well as Europe or farther regions. Dongyang refers to Japan.

石碑，是中古两国友好的历史见证。郑和七次出使西洋，每次都到古里。古里也不断派遣使者访问中国。

郑和率领船队回航途中访问了旧港。旧港又作巨港(今属印度尼西亚)，明朝人称之为三佛齐国，在苏门答腊岛的东北部。明初，不少华人下南洋到三佛齐。如广东南海人梁道明到三佛齐后，闽粤两省数千下南洋者投奔梁道明，公推他为酋长。三佛齐另一个头目是华侨陈祖义，原是广东潮州的一个恶霸，后来成为三佛齐酋长之一。他常在海面上聚众抢劫来往船只和客商，成了海盗。1407年，陈祖义得知郑和船队要来旧港，猜想船上宝物一定不少，于是便暗中策划劫掠。

南洋

南洋是明、清时期对东南亚一带的称呼，是以中国为中心的一个概念。包括马来群岛、菲律宾群岛、印度尼西亚群岛，也包括中南半岛沿海、马来半岛等地。中国明朝时期及明亡后，大量汉族移民涌入该区域谋生、定居，叫做"下南洋"。

南洋概念与西洋、东洋、北洋相对应。西洋指马六甲海峡以西的印度洋地区，还包括欧洲或更远的地方；东洋特指日本。

37

plan against the fleet. On the night when Chen Zuyi met with Zheng He, the wind was strong, the black clouds rolled and everything was dark. Chen Zuyi believed that it was the best time to attack Zheng He's fleet, and led his pirate vessels towards the fleet. As they got closer, Chen Zuyi discovered that all the lights on the fleet had been turned off. On discovering the darkness, many of the pirates thought Zheng He had already made preparations and became nervous. Chen Zuyi encouraged the pirates, saying the fleet had put out the lights and fallen asleep. He pushed forward. As they reached the fleet, Zheng He, who had made full preparations, gave an order to fire spears. Some of Chen Zuyi's subordinates fell into the sea while others sought to escape. At that time, Zheng He's seamen lit torches and surrounded the pirate vessels, giving them no way to escape. Brave seamen rushed to the pirate vessels. After a close fight, some pirates were killed and others captured. More than 5,000 pirates were killed, 10 pirate vessels destroyed and another seven vessels were captured. Three leaders of the pirates including Chen Zuyi were captured. They were later sent back to Nanjing and put to death. It was the first time Zheng He had to use arms in one of his expeditions and did so with complete success.

In fighting the pirates, Zheng He removed an obstacle to safe and smooth sea travel. People living in

　　另一个爱国华侨广东人施进卿，平日极恨陈祖义的海盗行径。郑和船队到来后，他立即把陈祖义的阴谋报告郑和。郑和想争取陈祖义改邪归正，向他宣读了明朝皇帝的国书；同时也作好充分的防卫准备。陈祖义当面表示友好，暗地里仍在打船队的主意。就在他同郑和见面的当天夜里，海风大作，乌云翻滚，一片漆黑。陈祖义认为这是动手偷袭的好时机，便悄悄率领海盗船驶近郑和船队。距离越来越近，看得见船队的所有灯光都已熄灭。目睹此状，不少匪徒估计郑和也许有了准备，不禁害怕起来。陈祖义则给匪徒打气说：人家熄灯睡觉了，大家还不快上！于是海盗们加快划船，靠拢船队。当匪徒们快接近船队时，早有准备的郑和一声号令，火铳齐发，霎时烟雾弥漫，火光映天，铁砂如雨，只见陈祖义的部众有的翻落海中，有的掉头想逃。此时，郑和船队队员们点亮火把，包围了海盗船，使陈祖义一伙海盗无路可逃。勇敢的船员奋不顾身地冲上海盗船，一阵厮杀，匪徒有的被打死，有的被活捉。这一仗，共杀死海盗5000余人，烧毁海盗船10艘，缴获7艘，活捉陈祖义等头目3人，后押回京师南京处斩。这是郑和下西洋首次用

surrounding areas clapped their hands and praised Zheng He's actions. People in Sanfoqi elected Shi Jinqing as their leader to manage local affairs. The Ming Dynasty Government conferred the title of Jiugang Xuanweishi to Shi Jinqing. Xuanweishi was an official position set up by the Government of the Ming Dynasty among minority nationalities and remote areas. The Xuanweishi was in charge of military and civil affairs. The position was usually assumed by local people. Jiugang Xuanweishi was the only administrative institute of the Ming Dynasty in Southeast Asia. At that time, the relationship between Jiugang and the Ming Dynasty became closer than with any other overseas countries and became subsidiary in nature.

On Sept. 21, 1407 (the second day of September in the traditional Chinese calendar), Zheng He returned to Nanjing after completing his first voyage to the western oceans. The voyage lasted more than two years. Emperor Yongle rewarded soldiers and officials that served with distinction and congratulated all members of the fleet.

The second voyage to the western oceans (1407–1409)

In order to establish friendly relationships with more overseas countries, Emperor Yongle ordered Zheng He to prepare for the second voyage after resting in Nanjing for

兵，结果大获全胜。

郑和为海路的安全和畅通除掉了一大害，附近地区人民无不拍手称快，感谢郑和果断除盗的义举。三佛齐人民拥戴为人正派的施进卿为当地酋长，管理当地军民大事。明朝政府敕封其为旧港宣慰使。宣慰使是明朝政府在少数民族和边远地区设置的掌管军民事务的官职，多由地方人士充任。旧港宣慰使司是明朝政府在东南亚地区唯一的行政机构。此时的旧港与明朝政府的关系，比海外各国更近一层，带有"内属"性质。

1407年9月21日（农历九月初二日），郑和圆满结束第一次下西洋回到南京，历时两年余。永乐皇帝奖赏有功将士并慰劳船队全体人员。

第二次下西洋（1407—1409）

郑和第一次下西洋后，永乐皇帝为了同更多的域外国家通好，即命郑和在南京休息十数日后，准备第二次下西洋。

1407年10月2日（农历九月十三日），郑和第二次率领船队下西洋。这次仍从太仓刘家港开航，至福建

a few days.

On October 2, 1407 (the 13th day of September of the Chinese traditional calendar), Zheng He launched the fleet in another voyage to the western oceans. This time, the fleet departed from Liujiagang in Taicang and berthed at the Taiping Port, Changle, Fujian for the monsoon. After the monsoon, the fleet sailed to the south and arrived in Zhancheng. Then, the fleet sailed to Java from Zhancheng.

This time, the main purpose for Zheng He's visit to Java was to collect 60,000 *liang* gold of compensation from the west king of Java for the wrongly killing Chinese seamen. However, the west king could not pay the compensation. He only paid 20,000 *liang* of gold, and 40,000 *liang* remained unpaid. Emperor Yongle said he would be satisfied as long as the west king realized his mistake and exempted the king from paying the rest. The king of west Java was awed by Zheng He's military forces and, in gratitude, was sincerely convinced. Java has kept friendly relationships with China since then and the resolution of the matter improved the reputation of China in Nanyang.

After the visit to Java, Zheng He's fleet sailed to Siam State (today's Thailand). Siam was a state that believed the Theravada Buddhism. There were plenty of temples in the country, which was known as the country of the 1,000 Buddhas.

Zheng He was warmly welcomed by the king of Siam

长乐太平港等候季风，季风来后再扬帆南下，首先到达占城，再由占城直赴爪哇国。

郑和到爪哇，主要使命之一是向西王收取误杀中国船员的赔款6万两黄金。而西王却因国力衰竭无力全部承担，仅交出2万两黄金谢罪，还差4万两。永乐皇帝说，只要知过而改就好了，于是免去所欠全部黄金。爪哇国西王既慑于郑和使团的武力，又感激永乐皇帝的恩德，自此心悦诚服，与中国一直保持着友好关系。这一事件的妥善解决，提高了中国在南洋地区的威望。

泰国古都大城府的"三宝公庙"。大城府位于曼谷以北80多公里，郑和船队通过河道直达这里。
Sanbao Temple in Ayutthaya, an ancient city in Thailand. Ayutthaya is more than 80 kilometers away to the north of Bangkok. Zheng He's fleet arrived here directly after passing the river course.

结束了对爪哇国的访问，郑和船队便到暹罗国（今泰国）访问。暹罗是个信仰小乘佛教的国家，国内寺庙众多，被誉为"千佛之国"。

郑和抵达暹罗时，受到暹罗国王的隆重欢迎。被欢迎的郑和端坐在锦缎绣制的罗伞下面，由伙役们

and was carried by servants on chair covered by an embroidered umbrella. The king of Siam threw a banquet to welcome Zheng He and talked about the friendly ties between the two countries. Zheng He dispatched people to teach advanced technologies such as wood cutting, ceramics making, salt shinning, well drilling and terrace exploration to local people, greatly benefiting the country. In order to extend his thanks to Zheng He, the king of Siam ordered the construction of a Zheng He temple and carved a 10-meter recumbent statue of Zheng He.

In Siam, Zheng He dispatched some vessels to visit Zhenla (today's Cambodia). The Chinese guests were warmly receipted by the king of Zhenla. The king told the Chinese envoys that when Zhancheng dispatched armies to attack them, the emperor of Ming Dynasty mediated between Zhancheng and their country, stopping the fighting and establishing friendly ties between the two countries. The king insisted that the people in Zhenla would not forget the favor.

After leaving Siam, Zheng He's fleet passed Manlajia and sailed westward to the Indian Ocean. The fleet arrived in Cochin (today's Cochin in India). Cochin was one of India's important ports for foreign trade at the time. Cochin has the Arabian Sea to the west, huge mountains to the east and borders on the sea in the west, south and north. Vessels of the fleet could easily arrive

抬着前进。国王在王宫设宴款待郑和，席间宾主畅叙两国友谊。郑和派人在暹罗传授伐木、烧制陶器、晒盐、凿井、开垦梯田等先进技术，使暹罗国受益匪浅。为感激郑和的恩德，暹罗国王下令建造一座郑和庙，雕塑一尊长10米的巨大的郑和卧像，因为佛教徒对卧像最为崇敬。

在暹罗，郑和分遣一部分船只前往真腊（今柬埔寨）访问。中国客人来到后，受到真腊国王热情欢迎。国王对中国使者说：占城出兵攻打我们，多亏大明皇帝出面调停，才使占城罢兵，并与我们和好；真腊人民永远不会忘记这一恩典。

离开暹罗后，郑和船队经满剌加继续向印度洋西行，抵达柯枝国（今印度科钦）。柯枝是印度古代对外贸易的重要港口之一；它西邻阿拉伯海，东连大山，西南北三面皆海，船队船只可以直达。当郑和船队抵达柯枝国海岸时，国王和居民拥立岸边，热烈欢迎中国客人。

柯枝国气候温润，雨量充沛，半年下雨半年晴。盛产胡椒，有"胡椒国"之称。胡椒、珍珠和宝石是其出口的三大产品。柯枝国商人用这些货物与郑和船

at Cochin. When Zheng He's fleet arrived at the beach of Cochin, the king and local residents of the country stood at the beaches and warmly welcomed the Chinese guests.

Cochin has a humid temperature and plenty of rainfall. About half of the days in any given year are rainy and the other half sunny. The country teems with spices and is known as the "the State of Spices." Spices, pearls and gems were the country's three major exports. Cochin businessmen traded with Zheng He's fleet.

After departing from Cochin, some of the vessels from Zheng He's fleet sailed to Ganbali (today's Cape Comarin on the southern tip of Indian Peninsula) and Ababadan (today's Ahmedabad, India) for a visit. Most of the vessels sailed southward to Xilanshan (today's Sri Lanka).

Xilanshan was called Simghala in ancient times. It was located in the sea to the south of the Indian Peninsula and was a communications center for offshore traffic between the Pacific Ocean and West Asia, Europe and Africa. It was a place had to be passed by east-to-west shipping lines. In its first voyage, Zheng He's fleet arrived in Xilanshan. The king of Xilanshan was arrogant and wanted to take advantage of Zheng He. Zheng He felt this and decided to leave the country. Despite this, Zheng He still visited Xilanshan with a letter of credence from Emperor Yongle and gifts, hoping to establish friendly ties with the country. Zheng He gave gold and silver, silk, incense and

队进行交易。

郑和船队离开柯枝国后，分出部分船只至甘巴里（今印度半岛南端的科摩林角）、阿拔巴丹（今印度的阿默达巴德）进行访问，主船队则南下来到锡兰山（今斯里兰卡）访问。

锡兰山，为古代僧伽罗国，在印度半岛南面的大海之中，扼太平洋与西亚、欧非之间海上交通的要冲，是古代东西航线必经之道。郑和第一次下西洋时，船队就曾到达锡兰山，国王亚烈苦奈儿傲慢不

郑和第二次下西洋期间在锡兰山刊立的《布施碑》，现存于斯里兰卡首都科伦坡博物馆。
The Donation Stele set up by Zheng He in Ceylan in his second voyage to the western oceans. The Stele is now kept at the Colombo National Museum in the capital of Sri Lanka.

candles to many temples in the country, and set up a stone stele on the first day of February of 1409 in the traditional Chinese calendar. The Stele for Donation to Temples in Xilanshan was engraved in three languages—Chinese, Persian and Tamil. Besides recording the articles donated, the words in three different languages expressed praise from Zheng He and other envoys of the Ming Dynasty for their contributions to Buddhism, Islam and Hinduism.

The expression of praise to the three religions in three languages on one stele reflected Zheng He's respect to the religious belief of all western countries and his tenet of establishing a peaceful international environment and developing business and trade, promoting China and foreign economic and cultural exchanges by spreading the peaceful diplomatic policies of the Ming Dynasty through religious activities. The stele showcased the friendly policies of China in Ming Dynasty to the world and enhanced China's influence in overseas countries. The stele is now stored at the National Museum of Colombo in Sri Lanka.

After completing his visit to Xilanshan, Zheng He returned China through the Strait of Malacca and arrived in Nanjing in June 1409 of the traditional Chinese calendar. The voyage lasted one year and six to seven months.

恭，并欲加害郑和。郑和觉察后，隐忍而离去。尽管如此，此次郑和仍怀着睦邻友好的善良愿望，带着永乐皇帝的国书和布施的礼品来到锡兰山进行友好访问。郑和向该国多座佛寺布施了金钱银钱、丝绢绸缎、香炉蜡烛等物品，并于1409年农历二月初一日刻石立碑，以记其事。这块《布施锡兰山佛寺碑》用汉文、波斯文和泰米尔文三种文字镌刻。三种文字除同样记载布施的物品之外，还分别表达了郑和等中国明朝使臣对佛教、伊斯兰教和印度教功德的赞扬。

一块石碑上，用三种文字表达对三种宗教的颂扬，既表现了郑和对出使的西洋各国崇信宗教的尊重，也反映出郑和希冀通过宗教活动宣传明王朝的和平外交政策，建立和平安定的国际环境和发展商贸、促进中外经济文化交流的主旨。这块石碑向世界显示了明代中国的富有与奉行的睦邻友好的政策，扩大了中国在海外各国的影响。此石碑现存于斯里兰卡科伦坡博物馆。

郑和结束锡兰山的访问后，经马六甲海峡返航回国，于1409年农历六月回到南京。此次历时约一年零六七个月。

The third voyage to the western oceans (1409–1411)

In his first two voyages, Zheng He established friendly ties with many countries in Southeast Asia. Aiming to reinforce and develop those ties, Emperor Yongle had started planning a third voyage before Zheng He returned from his second. Shortly after Zheng He's return to Nanjing, he started the third voyage with more than 27,000 seamen, 48 large vessels and more than 100 other vessels.

That September, Zheng He's fleet departed from the Liujiagang Port and arrived at the Taiping Port, in Changle, Fujian Province. In December, the fleet sailed from Wuhumen. A total of 48 huge vessels with 12 sails each sailed for 12 days and arrived in the Xinzhou Port of Zhancheng (in today's Quy Nhon, Vietnam). At that time, the Government of Ming Dynasty had successfully stopped an invasion to Zhancheng by Annan and helped Zhancheng take back the lands occupied by Annan. Therefore, the king of Zhancheng led officials of the country to welcome the envoys from the Ming Dynasty outside the city. The king wore gold flower crowns on his head and five-colored dresses, rode a huge elephant and was surrounded by an honor guard of over 500 people. Some members of the honor guard held swords and spears, some waved leather plates, some beat drums

第三次下西洋（1409—1411）

郑和两次下西洋之后，东南亚许多国家与中国建立了友好关系。为了巩固和发展这些关系，永乐皇帝在郑和第二次下西洋回国前，就确定了第三次下西洋的计划，并为此作好了各项准备。郑和回到南京没有休息多久，便于1409年农历九月统领船员27000余人，驾驶大型宝船48艘及其他船只100多艘第三次出使西洋。

当年九月，郑和船队从刘家港出发，十月到达福建长乐太平港，十二月从五虎门扬帆出海，每艘挂帆12张的巨大宝船48艘顺风疾驶12个昼夜，首站仍抵占城国的新州港（今越南归仁）。此时，明朝政府已成功制止了安南对占城的侵略，帮助占城收复了被安南侵占的大片土地。所以占城国王亲率大小官员出城迎接明朝使者。国王头戴三山金花冠，身穿五色礼服，披着锦花毛巾，骑着大象，前后簇拥着500多人的仪仗队。他们有的手拿刀枪，有的舞着皮牌、捶着鼓，有的吹起柳笛，向使团表达敬意和欢迎；欢乐情景胜过节日。当郑和向国王宣读永乐皇帝的诏书，并对国王和其属臣进行赏赐时，占城国王恭敬地翻身下象接受

and others played the flute to express their respect and welcome the envoys. When Zheng He announced the imperial decrees of Emperor Yongle and gave gifts to the king and officials, the king of Zhancheng got off the elephant and accepted the gifts deferentially. A grand welcome ceremony was then held at the palace. According to local tradition, people drank with bamboo suckers around a big vat and talked about the friendship of the two countries.

Zheng He's fleet then left Zhancheng for a visit to Zhenla. The fleet also visited the Angkor Ancient Relics 240 kilometers away from Phnompenh and learnt much about Buddhist architecture. These trips later provided an important reference to Zheng He's construction of the Nanjing Grand Bao'en Temple and the Glazed Pagoda when he governed Nanjing.

Zheng He's fleet left Zhenla and sailed southward. After a short visit to Temasek (today's Singapore), the fleet turned and sailed westward and arrived in Manlajia.

At that time, Manlajia held a cargo warehouse for Zheng He's fleet and was a base for long-distance navigation for the fleet. After a short rest in Manlajia, the fleet sailed westward and passed Aru, Sumatra and Nanwuli. Then, the fleet was divided into two. One part sailed to Jiayile (in today's southeast tip of India), Ababadan and Ganbali. The other part, led by Zheng He,

东埔寨吴哥寺
Angkor Wat in Cambodia

赏赐。继而在王宫举行盛大欢迎宴会，按当地风俗，围着大瓮用竹制吸管开怀畅饮美酒，共叙两国友谊。

郑和船队离开占城又到真腊访问，并去距金边240公里的吴哥古迹考察参观，获得不少佛教建筑知识。这为郑和后来任南京守备期间主持兴建南京大报恩寺及琉璃宝塔提供了重要参考。

郑和船队离开真腊，向南航行，在淡马锡（今新加坡）作短暂访问，即折向西行，到达满剌加。

满剌加这时已成为郑和船队的货物仓库，是郑和船队继续远航的途中基地。在满剌加作了短暂休

sailed to Xiaogelan, Cochin, Xilanshan and Calicut. The team returned back after a visit to Guli.

In 1410, Zheng He visited Xilanshan again in his return voyage. When visiting Xilanshan in his first voyage, Zheng He tried to resolve issues in a peaceful manner. However, things went contrary to his wishes. The king of Xilanshan didn't listen to Zheng He's arguments and planed to do harm to Zheng He and the fleet, so Zheng He left the country. In his second visit to Xilanshan, not enough time had passed and no issues had been solved. Zheng He knew about the king's greed and cruelty and believed that if the issues could not be solved, it would be difficult for him to open a sea route to the west. Therefore, he returned the case to Emperor Yongle after returning to China. With the support of Emperor Yongle, Zheng He visited Xilanshan a third time. The king of Xilanshan invited Zheng He to visit his palace but plotted to capture Zheng He to ask for a ransom. The king also dispatched 50,000 soldiers to the seaside to attack and rob the vessels of Ming Dynasty. The king also cut trees and set them up as barriers to block Zheng He's return route. But Zheng He was aware of the potential for treachery and took a force of 3,000 to follow him. After arriving at the palace, Zheng He announced the imperial decree of Emperor Yongle and gave gifts to the king as usual and tried to persuade him to give up evil ways. The king refused

整后，郑和船队继续西行，经阿鲁、苏门答剌、南巫里，然后分成两路：一路向加异勒（今印度东南端）、阿拔巴丹和甘巴里驶去；另一路由郑和率领向小葛兰、柯枝、锡兰山、古里进发。访问古里后即返航。

1410年，郑和在返航途中再赴锡兰山。郑和第一次下西洋访问锡兰山时，曾试图以和平方式解决锡兰山问题，但事与愿违，国王亚烈苦奈儿非但不听忠告，反而阴谋加害郑和。郑和第二次出使锡兰山，时机不成熟，问题仍未能解决。郑和深知亚烈苦奈儿的贪婪和凶暴，如不解决这一问题，则难以打通向西远航的海路。郑和回国后向永乐皇帝禀报了这一情况。在永乐皇帝的支持下，郑和第三次奉命出使锡兰山。亚烈苦奈儿一面假惺惺地邀请郑和一行到他宫中作客，阴谋俘获郑和，借以勒取赎金；一面暗中兵发5万到海边，阴谋袭劫明朝宝船，夺取钱财；另又伐木设障，以断绝郑和一行的归路，使之互相不得救援。郑和对其已有觉察，提高了警惕，所以加派3000人的武装卫队随行。到达王宫以后，郑和照例向亚烈苦奈儿宣读永乐皇帝的诏书，赠送礼品，并直言相陈，再次

to accept Zheng He's persuasion and ordered his son to ask for treasures from Zheng He. Zheng He refused his request with stern words and left in anger. On the way back to the fleet, Zheng He found that his way was blocked. In these dangerous circumstances, Zheng He was calm and made immediate arrangements. He asked others to return to the fleet from other roads to order officials and soldiers of the fleet to fight bravely. He then led his armed escort of 3,000 to attack the city of Xilanshan from byways and captured the king of Xilanshan and his family members. The armies of Xilanshan, sent to rob Zheng He's fleet, returned to the city in a hurry after hearing the news and surrounded the imperial city of Xilanshan. Zheng He and his escort held the imperial city and fought with the armies of Xilanshan for six nights. On one morning, Zheng He and his escort took the king of Xilanshan and other prisoners and, at dawn, and broke through the tight encirclement. With the help of officers and soldiers of the fleet, they fought till the evening, and eventually defeated the armies of Xilanshan and returned to the fleet.

When Zheng He returned after this third voyage, friendly envoys from 19 countries followed Zheng He's fleet to visit China.

On June 16, 1411 of the traditional Chinese calendar, Zheng He's fleet returned to Nanjing with friendly envoys from 19 countries and the captured king of Xilanshan. The

要求亚烈苦奈儿改恶从善。亚烈苦奈儿不但拒不接受规劝，还令其子纳颜向郑和勒索金银宝物。郑和当即严词拒绝，并愤然告辞。在回船队的途中，郑和发觉道路已被阻绝。在这十分危急的情况下，郑和镇定自若，迅速作出处置，派人由其他道路回到船队，命令船队官兵立即奋勇抗击，自己则率卫队3000人，由小道夜袭锡兰王城，生擒亚烈苦奈儿及其家属、头目多人。前往劫夺郑和船队的锡兰军队闻讯，急匆匆赶回救援，包围锡兰王城。郑和等人坚守不出，如此反复攻战六个昼夜。一日清晨，郑和等人押着亚烈苦奈儿等，趁着微曦打开城门，冲出重围，且战且进，在船队官兵的接应下，激战至黄昏，终于打退锡兰军队的追击，胜利返回船队。

郑和访问南洋浮雕
Relievo of Zheng He's voyage to Nanyang

third voyage lasted for one year and eight months. Foreign envoys were warmly receipted by the Government of the Ming Dynasty. The king of Xilanshan waited for disposal by Emperor Yongle. In consideration of the friendly ties between China and Xilanshan and the blindness of the king, Emperor Yongle determined to remit the punishment but removed his post as king of Xilanshan. He ordered the king to live in China temporarily and sought to find a talented relative to set up as the new king. On July 13, 1412 of the Chinese traditional calendar, Emperor Yongle dispatched envoys to visit Xilanshan with his imperial decrees and seal, and appointed a new king. In the meantime, the former king was sent back to the country.

The solution of the Xilanshan issue laid the basis for peace between eastern and western countries in the west oceans and removed the barriers for the "Maritime Silk Road" and for trade between countries in Asia and Africa.

The fourth voyage to the western oceans (1413–1415)

Zheng He's first three voyages to the western oceans all ended in Calicut, without reaching beyond South and Southeast Asia. The main tasks of the voyages were to open a route between China and the Indian Peninsula, establish the reputation of the Ming Dynasty in these

郑和第三次下西洋归来时，随同郑和船队到中国访问的，有19个国家的友好使者。

1411年农历六月十六日，郑和船队带着19个国家的友好使者，押着一个锡兰王亚烈苦奈儿，回到南京。第三次下西洋历时一年八个月。外国友好使者受到明王朝政府的热烈欢迎和盛情款待；被羁押的锡兰山王则等候永乐皇帝的处置。永乐皇帝为了中锡两国友谊，并念其愚昧无知，决定予以赦免；但废除了他的锡兰王位，让其暂时住在中国。同时，命礼部在亚烈苦奈儿的亲属中选贤能者为锡兰山国王。礼部奉命选耶巴乃那为王位继承者。1412年农历七月十三日，永乐皇帝遣使携带诏书及诰印前往锡兰山，册封耶巴乃那为国王，亚烈苦奈儿亦同时被遣返回国。

锡兰山问题的解决，奠定了当时西洋和平安定的局面，使亚非各国之间往来交通的"海上丝绸之路"完全畅通无阻。

第四次下西洋（1413—1415）

郑和前三次下西洋，都是以古里国为终点，足迹限于东南亚和南亚，其主要任务是打通中国到印度

regions and set up a transfer base for expeditions to regions west of South Asia. All these tasks were successfully completed after three voyages and Zheng He also accumulated rich sailing experience. By that time, the reign of Emperor Yongle entered a golden age and the country became even stronger. Therefore, Emperor Yongle ordered Zheng He to make a fourth expedition to reach the unknown Muslim world west of South Asia.

The fourth voyage to the western oceans marked a new phase in Zheng He's marine activities. He spent more time conditioning and preparing than for the first three. This time he was to visit countries and regions of the Arab World where people believed in Islam. To cope with the daunting task of translation and interpreting, Zheng He made a special trip to Xi'an and invited Hasan, Imam of the Great Mosque of Yangshi, who knew Arabic, and invited him to go along. Before setting out, Zheng He asked for Emperor Yongle's approval to build a Tianfei Palace in Changle, Fujian, for the worship of Goddess Tianfei, or Mazu, who protected seafarers and fishermen.

In January, 1513, Zheng He started his fourth voyage, commanding a massive fleet. Following the old route, he arrived in Sumatra after passing Champa, Java, Palembang, Malacca, Pahang and Kelantan. Located in the northwest of Sumatra Island, with seas in the north and mountains in the south, the country of Sumatra served as

半岛的航路，在这一带地区树立明王朝的声威，同时也为向南亚以西地区远航建立中转基地。通过三次出使，郑和已圆满完成了上述任务，并积累了丰富的航海经验。此时，永乐朝进入了鼎盛时期，国力更加雄厚。为此，永乐皇帝命令郑和第四次出使西洋，向南亚以西未知的伊斯兰世界挺进。

第四次下西洋标志郑和航海活动进入了新阶段，所以出使前的休整及准备的时间较之前三次都长。这次计划访问的国家和地区属阿拉伯世界，人们都信奉伊斯兰教，翻译任务十分繁重。为此，郑和专程赶往陕西，求得通晓阿拉伯语的西安羊市大清真寺掌教哈三同行。远航前夕，他奏请永乐皇帝准予在福建长乐兴建天妃宫以祭祀海神天妃（妈祖），祈求保佑航海平安。

1513年1月，郑和率领庞大船队开始第四次出访，沿着旧路，经占城、爪哇、旧港、满剌加、彭亨、急兰丹等国到达苏门答剌。苏门答剌国位于今苏门答腊岛西北部，北临大海，南靠大山，为从南海通往印度洋的海上东西交通孔道。郑和船队在这里设有"官厂"（货物转运站），储存船队与各国贸易的货物以

a maritime transport channel linking the South China Sea and the Indian Ocean. There Zheng He's fleet had a "state plant" (cargo transfer station) which stored goods traded between the fleet and the foreign countries, as well as all kinds of necessities for the fleet. This station was to play a very important role in Zheng He's future foreign visits.

When Zheng He's fleet arrived in Sumatra, the country was torn by civil strife. Under orders from Emperor Yongle, Zheng He's fleet interfered in the strife and put an end to it. The story goes like this. The former king of Sumatra was attacked by the king of Nakur, a country to the west. The Sumatran king was killed by a poisoned arrow in the fight, and half of Sumatra's land was taken over by Nakur. As the prince of Sumatra was too young to seek revenge for his father's death, the queen of Sumatra vowed in public that she would marry whoever could avenge her husband, recover the lost land and manage the country. A fisherman answered her call, saying that he could avenge the king's death. With the army under his command, the fisherman fought bravely against the enemy. He recovered the lost land and killed the king of Nakur. The queen, living up to her promise, married the fisherman and made him king of Sumatra. In 1409, the fisherman king dispatched an envoy and paid tribute to the Ming Dynasty. Three years later, however, the prince of Sumatra grew up. He conspired with officials who were

及船队所需的各种备用物品。在郑和下一阶段的对外交往中，其地位显得十分重要。

　　郑和船队抵达苏门答剌时，正逢该国发生内乱。郑和奉永乐皇帝之命一举平定之，情况如下：苏门答剌前国王受西面那孤儿国的花面王攻击，在抗战时中毒箭而死，国土也被那孤儿国占去了一大半。这时王子锁丹罕难阿必镇尚幼，还不能为父报仇；苏门答剌王后则当众宣誓，能替我丈夫报仇、收复国土者，我愿以身相许，做他的妻子，和他共同管理国事。此时，有一个渔翁出来说道：我能替王后报仇。于是，渔翁率领军队勇敢作战，果然收复失地，杀死了花面王。王后不负前盟，做了渔翁的妻子。这个渔翁就成了苏门答剌的国王。1409年，渔翁王曾遣使向明朝进贡方物。三年后，先王子锁丹罕难阿必镇长大成人，与反对渔翁王的部将合谋，将其义父渔翁王杀死，夺取了王位。渔翁王的儿子苏干剌见此情状不得不率众逃入山中，自立为王并不断向先王之子发起攻击。1413年，锁丹罕难阿必镇又遣使向明朝求援，永乐皇帝答应了他的请求，于是命令郑和第四次下西洋时出兵相助。

against the fisherman king and killed his stepfather for the throne. The son of the fisherman was forced to retreat into the mountains. There, he made himself king and launched continuous attacks on the son of the former king. In 1413, the son of the former king sent an envoy to the Ming Dynasty and asked for help. Emperor Yongle granted his request and ordered Zheng He to give him a hand during the fourth voyage to the western oceans.

When Zheng He first arrived in Sumatra, he did not bother to interfere in the war. Instead, he presented his credentials to the king of Sumatra, bestowed gifts at court and conducted trade with the country as usual. The son of the fisherman king was annoyed by Zheng He's seemingly normal practices. Displeased that Zheng He did not present him with any gifts, the fisherman's son attacked Zheng He. Zheng He's fleet fought back in self-defense and collaborated with the force of the Sumatran king. After a fierce battle, the fisherman's son was defeated and fled to Lambri. Zheng He's army was in hot pursuit and did not withdraw until the son and his wife were captured alive. The two of them were sent back to China where Emperor Yongle ordered the Ministry of Justice to put the son to death.

After the problem of Sumatra was brilliantly and completely settled, Zheng He divided his fleet into two, one part would head westward to explore routes along

印尼苏门答腊岛亚齐的郑和大钟
Giant Bell of Zheng He at Aceh in Sumatra,
Indonesia

郑和来到苏门答剌，没有急于动手，按惯例向国王递交国书，进行赏赐和贸易。对于郑和这些看来十分平常的举动，苏干剌却非常不满，恨郑和没有赏赐给他，于是带领部下数万人前来攻打郑和。郑和以自卫反击的方式，与国王锁丹罕难阿必镇的军队配合，与之展开激战。苏干剌战败逃亡南渤利国。郑和穷追不舍，直至将苏干剌及其妻子俘获方才收兵，将其押回中国，交由永乐皇帝圣裁。永乐皇帝命刑部将苏干剌处斩。

郑和在干净彻底解决苏干剌问题以后，分出船队向西探测赴非洲大陆东岸的航路，大部分船队则经锡兰、加异勒到达古里。在古里稍事休整，就向西横穿阿拉伯海，向对岸波斯湾的忽鲁谟斯驶去。

印度洋是世界四大洋之一，位处赤道，气候炎热且变化无常。有时晴空万里，波平如镜；有时乌云翻滚，恶浪如山。郑和船队在驶向忽鲁谟斯途中，就遭遇一次飓风的袭击。其时，汹涌的波涛像海妖水怪一

the east coast of Africa and the majority would head for Calicut through Ceylon and Jiayile. After a short break in Calicut, the fleet crossed the Arabian Sea in the west and headed towards Hormuz on the other side of the Persian Gulf.

The Indian Ocean is one of the four great oceans of the world. Located close to the equator, the Indian Ocean is hot and volatile. Sometimes the clear sky spreads over ten thousand miles and the sea is smooth as a mirror; other times, the whole sky is covered with black clouds and the sea turns ferocious with waves reaching enormous heights. Zheng He's fleet was hit by a hurricane on its way to Hormuz. Surging waves rushed Zheng He's fleet like monsters. The sea water became pitch black. Roaring thunder and lightning hit the fleet in the face. Some of the masts broke and some of the ship plates rattled—the ships were in danger of capsizing at any minute. Although the fleet had met a lot of fierce storms in previous voyages, none was as ferocious as this one. Zheng He did not panic; he was calm and collected. He knew the power of the gods could help clear the horror and restore confidence when people were terrified by unknown terror.

With this idea in mind, he ordered a red light be put on top of the ship. The red light shimmered in the storm, looking very attractive in the dark. Zheng He shouted, "Goddess Tianfei is here!" Everyone in the fleet fixed their

齐向郑和船队扑来，海水霎时变得墨黑，巨雷夹着闪电劈头盖脸地轰将过来。有的桅杆被折断了，有的船板发出嘎嘎的响声，随时有被风浪掀翻沉海的危险。虽说前几次航行狂风恶浪经历不少，可都没有这次来得猛烈。郑和不慌不乱，表现沉着。他知道，当人们面对一种不可知的恐怖而心慌意乱时，最好的办法是借助神的力量，使大家清除恐怖，恢复信心。想到此，他差人在船的最高处点起一盏红灯。这红色灯光在风暴中闪烁不定，在黑暗中极富诱惑力。他大喊一声，"天妃娘娘显灵啦！"随着他的呐喊，船上所有人的目光都集中到这神秘的红灯上，一种得救的心情弥漫开来。好多人跪下来向天妃膜拜。甚至有人说，自己不但看到了神灯，还影影绰绰地看到了天妃。

"天妃娘娘显灵"这一振奋人心的喜讯，随着船上全体人员的欢呼，由近及远，传遍整个船队。郑和抓住时机，用坚定和充满信心的声调，向全体人员喊道："天妃娘娘最喜欢勇敢的弄潮人，我们应该尽快行动起来，抗击风暴，报答天妃娘娘的庇佑！"人们的信心恢复了，腿脚也不软了，各就各位，投入抗击风暴的战斗。这时虽大雨滂沱，但风势却逐渐减弱，浪也

eyes on the mysterious red light at Zheng He's shout and they saw the light of hope shining. Many knelt down and prayed to the Goddess Tianfei. Some even said that they saw not only the heavenly light but also a vague image of the Goddess herself. The good news about the arrival of Goddess Tianfei spread across the entire fleet as crew members shouted and acclaimed. Zheng He took the opportunity and said to everyone in a firm and confident voice, "Goddess Tianfei prefers sailors who are brave. Let's work together to fight against the storm and repay the blessings bestowed unto us by Goddess Tianfei!" The sailors' confidence was restored, and they regained their strength. Everyone assumed his own position and threw himself into the fight against the hurricane. The rain remained heavy, but the wind and the waves began to die down. Zheng He's fleet braved the storm and traveled 25 days and nights without stopping. Eventually, they crossed the Arabian Sea, entered the Persian Gulf, and reached their destination, Hormuz (Kishm, the biggest island in the Strait of Hormuz; today's Iran port).

Hormuz was a big country near the Arabian Peninsula. It had become an important trade port since the second half of the 13th century. People traveling between the east and the west, be they traveling by land or by sea, had to pass through Hormuz. The Hormuz people, including the king, were all believers in Islam. Mosques were found

忽鲁谟斯（今霍尔木兹海峡）
Hormuz (the Hormuz Strait at present)

小多了。郑和船队顶风冒雨，战风斗浪，昼夜兼程，经过25个昼夜，穿过阿拉伯海进入波斯湾，最后到达目的地忽鲁谟斯（霍尔木兹海峡中最大的岛格什姆岛，今伊朗海港）。

忽鲁谟斯（霍尔木兹）是郑和越过阿拉伯海到达的阿拉伯半岛附近的一个西洋大国。从13世纪下半叶以来，这里就是重要贸易港口。往来于东西交通的人们，不论是陆路或是海港，都要由此通过。这里上自国王、下至百姓都崇奉伊斯兰教，国内清真寺众多，其文武医卜和各色技艺都很发达，胜过其他西洋国家。

almost everywhere and the country had better culture, medicine and craftsmanship than any other country in the western ocean.

After Zheng He arrived in Hormuz, the king held a grand welcome ceremony for him at the royal palace. The host and the guest exchanged gifts and had a friendly talk. To see for himself the beautiful scenery of the country and to learn about the local customs and products, Zheng He's mission paid a visit to the downtown areas. There they saw magnificent mosques, luxurious streets and a rich variety of products which attracted visitors from all parts of the world. All kinds of food—roasted lamb, roasted chicken, roasted beef, thin pancakes, fried twists—were on the shelves, but not a single wine shop was found, because drinking wine was prohibited in the country. The people were simple and honest. If one family suffered disasters or poverty, everyone would lend a helping hand by offering food, clothes and money.

When the people of Hormuz heard about the arrival of Zheng He's fleet from China, they ran around spreading the news, and sought to trade for China's silk, chinaware and tea with amber, coral, opal, pearl and medicine.

When Zheng He started his trip back home, the king of Hormuz loaded the ships with a lot of rare animals, including kylins (giraffes), lions, ostriches, antelopes, zebras, as well as pearl and precious stones. He also sent

当郑和抵达忽鲁谟斯国时，国王在王宫里举行隆重的欢迎仪式，宾主双方互赠礼品，并进行了友好的会谈。

为一睹这西洋大国的旖旎风光和了解当地的物产民情，郑和使团特意到市内走访。只见这里有宏大的清真寺、繁华的街市，五光十色的商品吸引着各方游客。烧羊、烧鸡、烧肉、薄饼、哈喇徹等荤肴面食应有尽有，但没有一家酒店，因为这里法律规定禁止饮酒。这里民风淳朴，一家遇难致贫，众人齐助以粮食、衣服、钱财。

忽鲁谟斯人得知中国郑和船队到来，奔走相告，并用琥珀、珊瑚、猫眼石、宝石和药材等物，来交换丝绸、瓷器、茶叶等中国商品。

郑和回国时，忽鲁谟斯国王派使臣己即丁带着国王的亲笔信，用船装着麒麟（即长颈鹿）、狮子、鸵鸟、羚羊、斑马、珍珠、宝石等，随郑和船队回访中国。郑和船队回国途中顺访溜山国（今马尔代夫群岛）。溜山国盛产龙涎香、乳香、椰子等物，百姓信奉伊斯兰教。郑和船队在这里收购龙涎香、椰子等物带回国内。

an envoy with a personal letter to pay a return visit to China with Zheng He's fleet. On their way back home, Zheng He's fleet dropped by the Country of Liushan (today's Maldives Islands). The country was abundant with ambergris, frankincense and coconut, and people there believed in Islam. Zheng He's fleet bought a lot of ambergris and coconut and brought them back to China.

The fourth voyage to the western oceans lasted a year and a half. Zheng He's fleet returned to Nanjing on August 12, 1415 (July 8 of the traditional Chinese calendar).

Zheng He reported his mission in detail to Emperor Yongle, including the fight against the hurricane. Emperor Yongle spoke highly of the courage exhibited by the members of Zheng He's fleet who put an end to the civil strife in Sumatra and fought against the hurricane in the Indian Ocean.

In memory of Zheng He's fourth voyage to the western oceans, Emperor Yongle issued an order to build a stele at the Tianfei Palace outside Fengyi Gate of the city of Nanjing. He composed the inscription on the stele on the sixth day of April of 1416, according to the Chinese lunar calendar.

The fourth voyage was a link between the previous trips and the expeditions to come. The fleet's trip to Hormuz marked a great shift from the first three voyages

第四次下西洋历时一年半。郑和船队于1415年8月12日（农历七月八日）回到南京。

郑和向永乐皇帝详细汇报了这次出使的情况及战胜风暴的经过。永乐皇帝对郑和船队全体人员在平息苏门答剌内乱和搏击印度洋风浪中所表现出来的英勇精神大加赞赏。

为纪念郑和第四次下西洋，永乐皇帝下令在南京仪凤门外天妃宫内刻立《御制弘仁普济天妃宫之碑》，并于1416年农历四月初六日亲撰碑文。

郑和船队远航忽鲁谟斯是对前三次下西洋的一大发展，也是对其后三次下西洋的一大推进。第四次下西洋具有承上启下的性质。

第五次下西洋（1417—1419）

经过郑和四次下西洋，中国明朝在东南亚、南亚、西亚乃至东非的影响越来越大，许多国家派使臣前来中国访问。1417年初，古里、爪哇、占城、锡兰山、卜剌哇、阿丹、苏门答剌、麻林、剌撒、忽鲁谟斯、柯枝、南巫里、沙里湾泥、彭亨等18个国家及旧港宣慰使司的使臣向永乐皇帝辞行。永乐皇帝派郑和

to the western oceans and was a starting point for the next three expeditions further into the world.

The fifth voyage to the western oceans (1417–1419)

After Zheng He's four trips to the western oceans, the Ming Dynasty's influence in Southeast Asia, South Asia, West Asia and even Eastern Africa was on the rise. Many countries sent their envoys to China. In early 1417, envoys from 18 countries, including Calicut, Java, Champa, Ceylon, Brava, Aden, Sumatra, Malindi, Ra's, Hormuz, Cochin, Indonesia, Singosari, and Pahang, along with envoys from the Palembang Pacification Commission, bid their goodbyes to Emperor Yongle. Emperor Yongle dispatched Zheng He to escort the envoys home and to present the kings of these countries with imperial edicts from the Ming Government and a variety of gifts. Therefore, Zheng He went on his fifth voyage to the western oceans in May of 1417, according to the Chinese lunar calendar.

Before the fleet left the country, Zheng He paid a visit to the tombs of Islamic sages in Lingshan Mountain outside the Renfeng Gate (East Gate) of Quanzhou, Fujian. On the one hand, he prayed for the blessings of Islamic sages; on the other hand, he wanted to pay tribute to the Arab sages who made contributions to the friendship between

护送各国使臣回国，并带明朝政府诏书及礼品，前往赏赐各国国王。于是，郑和奉命于1417年农历五月率领船队第五次出使西洋。

船队离国前，郑和一行曾去福建泉州仁凤门（东门）外灵山向伊斯兰教先贤墓行香，一方面祈求伊斯兰教先贤"灵圣庇佑"；另一方面，对曾为发展阿拉伯人民与中国人民之间的友谊作出贡献的阿拉伯先贤表示敬意。

郑和行香碑，位于福建泉州城东灵山圣墓的回廊西侧。灵山圣墓是伊斯兰教创始人穆罕默德的两位门徒的墓地，郑和第五次下西洋前到此行香。
Zheng He Pilgrimage Stele on the west side of the corridor of Lingshan Holy Tomb to the east of Quanzhou City, Fujian Province. The Lingshan Holy Tomb is the tomb of two disciples of Mohammed, the founder of Islamism. Zheng He visited the stele in his fifth voyage to the western oceans.

此次远航任务是护送18国使臣安全回国，航路由近及远：占城、爪哇、旧港、满剌加、彭亨、苏门答剌、南巫里、锡兰山、柯枝、古里、忽鲁谟斯、阿丹、木骨都束、卜剌哇、麻林。

阿丹国（今阿拉伯也门共和国之亚丁），位于阿拉伯半岛西南角，处在红海口上，是古代重要的国际贸易大港。该国气候温和，四季如春，土地肥沃，物产丰富。阿丹人信仰伊斯兰教，性格刚强，国势强盛，为近邻

Arabian and Chinese people.

The mission of this voyage was to escort the envoys from 18 countries back home. The fleet sailed to Champa, Java, Palembang, Malacca, Pahang, Sumatra, Indonesia, Ceylon, Cochin, Calicut, Hormuz, Aden, Mogadishu, Brava and Malindi.

Aden (now in the Yemen Arab Republic) was located at the southwest corner of the Arabian Peninsula, near the mouth of the Red Sea. It was an important international trade port in ancient times. The country enjoyed a mild climate, warm weather, fertile land and rich products. The people in Aden believed in Islam and had a strong character. Their country was so powerful that all neighboring countries were afraid of it. When Zheng He's fleet arrived in Aden, the king and his ministers waited at the seaside to greet Zheng He and held a grand welcome ceremony for him at the royal palace. Zheng He read out the imperial edict of Emperor Yongle, and presented the king with coins and gifts. In return, the Aden king offered Emperor Yongle a golden crown decorated with all kinds of pearl and precious stones.

Then, Zheng He's mission visited Ra's. The country was located to the west of Aden and the east of the Red Sea, close to the Lasa village of Mukalla of the Arabian Peninsula. People there lived in stone houses and there were three remarkable Islamic temples with round domes.

各国所畏惧。当郑和使团到达阿丹时，国王率领大臣到海边迎接，将郑和迎到王宫隆重接待。郑和宣读永乐皇帝国书，赠送彩币及礼品。阿丹国王回赠永乐皇帝一顶嵌有各种珍珠宝石的金冠。

接着，郑和使团访问剌撒。剌撒在阿丹以西，红海之东，阿拉伯半岛木卡拉（Mukalla）附近的Lasa村。其地倚海而居，垒石为屋，有三座引人注目的圆顶伊斯兰教寺院。郑和到此宣诏赐赏。1416年，该国曾遣使来中国进贡，以后又来中国三次，每次都与阿丹、卜剌哇使臣同行。郑和结束对剌撒的访问，过曼德海峡，向南航行，到达非洲东海岸的木骨都束、卜剌哇和麻林。

木骨都束（今索马里的摩加迪沙）山多地旷，雨量稀少，黄土赤石，田地贫瘠，收成很少。贫民出海捕鱼，富户则远出经商。这里产乳香、金钱豹、龙涎香。该国不产木材，居民多垒石为屋。

卜剌哇（今索马里东南岸布腊瓦）与木骨都束接壤，地多盐分，不能耕种，专靠捕鱼为生。

当郑和船队抵达非洲东部海域登岸踏上木骨都束和卜剌哇国土时，先后受到两国国王的热烈欢迎和盛

Zheng He announced the imperial edict there. In 1416, the country had sent envoys to China to pay tribute. Later, envoys from Ra's paid three visits to China, all accompanied by envoys from Aden and Brava. After Zheng He finished his visit to Ra's, his fleet passed the Bab el Mandeb Strait, and sailed southward to Mogaadicio, Brava and Malindi on the east coast of Africa.

Magaadicio (now Mogadishu in Somalia) was a mountainous country with little rainfall. With yellow soil and red stones, the fields there were barren with little harvest. Poor people went fishing in the sea, while those who were better-off went for business in faraway lands. The country was rich in frankincense, leopards and ambergris. Since it did not produce timber, most of the residents lived in stone houses.

Brava (now Brava on the southeast coast of Somalia) neighbored Magaadicio. Its lands were too salty for cultivation and people there had to rely on fishing for food and income.

When Zheng He's fleet arrived in the east coast of Africa and set foot on Magaadicio and Brava, they were warmly received by kings of the two countries. As usual, Zheng He announced the imperial edicts of Emperor Yongle to the two kings, and presented them with gifts. Before parting, the kings sent their envoys and gifts to China along with Zheng He's fleet. Among the gifts were

也门亚丁港
The Port of Aden in Yemen

情款待。郑和按例先后向两国国王宣读永乐皇帝的诏书，并赠送礼品。临别时，两国国王均派使臣携带礼物随郑和船队一道来中国访问。木骨都束国王还赠送瑞兽麒麟（长颈鹿）和狮子给明朝永乐皇帝。

郑和在东非的最后一站是麻林（即麻林地，今肯尼亚东岸马林迪），受到麻林国王热情款待。1415年麻林曾遣使献瑞兽麒麟，永乐皇帝及官员于京师皇宫奉天门隆重举行接受仪式。郑和船队本想继续南行，由于前方已接近奔巴岛、奔巴海峡，那里深林密布，杳无人烟，在当地人的劝阻下，乃于1419年春由麻林

an auspicious beast kylin (giraffe) and a lion from the king of Magaadicio to Emperor Yongle.

Zheng He's last stop in Eastern Africa was Malindi (now Malindi in the east coast of Kenya). There he was warmly received by the king. In 1415, Malindi sent envoys with an auspicious beast kylin to China and Emperor Yongle and his ministers held a grand reception ceremony for them at the Fengtian Gate of the royal court. Zheng He's fleet wanted to go even further to the south but they were already close to the Pemba Island and the Pemba Strait where there was nothing there but dense forests. Zheng He listened to the advice of local people and turned eastward to the Indian Ocean from Malindi in the spring of 1419. His fleet passed the Maldives, Ceylon, Sumatra and Malacca and returned to China in July. The voyage lasted for one year and nine months.

When Zheng He returned from his fifth voyage to the western oceans, he brought along envoys from 17 Asian and African countries, as well as many rare birds and animals, including ostriches from Hormuz, giraffes from Aden, giraffes and lions from Magaadicio, camels from Brava and Indian antelopes from Java.

The arrival of envoys from Asian and African countries and the presentation of rare birds and animals were the feature of Zheng He's fifth voyage to the western ocean.

肯尼亚马林迪把中国瓷器作为财富，瓷盘被当作珍贵的装饰镶在古墓上。
Malindi in Kenya takes Chinese porcelain as the fortune and the porcelain plate was imbedded on the tomb as precious decorations.

国向东横渡印度洋返航，经由溜山、锡兰山、苏门答刺、满刺加等地，于七月间回到国内，历时一年零九个月。

郑和第五次下西洋回国时，随船队来中国访问的有亚非17个国家的使臣及呈献的珍禽异兽。这些珍禽异兽有忽鲁谟斯的鸵鸟、阿丹的长颈鹿、木骨都束的长颈鹿和狮子、卜刺哇的骆驼、爪哇的麋里羔兽等。

郑和所访亚非国家的外交使臣纷沓而至及珍禽异兽的呈献，是第五次下西洋的特色。

The sixth voyage to the western oceans (1422–1423)

In 1421, Zheng He reached 50. In his first five voyages to the western oceans, he had become an experienced navigator. In the winter of that year, to escort envoys of 16 countries including Hormuz, Dhufar, Mogadishu, Ra's, Brava, Calicut, Cochin, Jiayile, Ceylon, Lambri, Sumatra, Aru, Malacca and Ganbali home, he was assigned to start his sixth voyage to the western oceans, bringing with him the state credentials of Emperor Yongle and a large number of gifts.

In the spring of 1422, Zheng He set out to sea, passing through numerous countries that he had already visited several times such as Champa, Siam, Malacca, Banggela, Ceylon, Cochin, Calicut, Ganbali, Suoli, Aden, Dhufar, Ra's, Mogadishu, Brava and Malindi. This time he also passed through places like Manbasa (today's Mombasa in Kenya) and Juba (known as Giumbo in Southern Somalia). Mombasa was located in the south of Malin, which indicates that Zheng He went even further in his sixth voyage, focusing mainly on visiting eastern African countries like Magadoxo, Malindi and Juba.

Zheng He reached countries along the east coast of Africa in his fifth and sixth voyages, which exerted a great influence on them. The kings all sought to establish relations with China, either by sending envoys to visit

第六次下西洋（1422—1423）

1421年，郑和已满50岁。经过五次下西洋的实践，他已成为一位具有丰富航海经验的航海家了。就在这年冬天，他奉命第六次下西洋，主要使命是护送忽鲁谟斯、祖法儿（位于今阿拉伯半岛西部沿岸的佐法儿，Dhufar）、木骨都束、剌撒、卜剌哇、古里、柯枝等16国使臣回国，并带永乐皇帝的国书和大批礼物备用。

郑和于1422年春出航，历经占城、暹罗、满剌加、锡兰山、古里、祖法儿、木骨都束、麻林等地，这都是他数经之地。这次出海，郑和还到了东非的慢八撒、竹步等地。慢八撒即今肯尼亚的著名海港蒙巴萨港，竹步即今索马里南部朱巴河口的准博（Giumbo）。慢八撒位于麻林之南，换言之，第六次下西洋航程比第五次更远，以东非国家木骨都束、麻林、竹步为访问重点。

郑和第五、六次下西洋，都到达非洲东岸诸国，对这个地区影响很大。许多国家纷纷与中国明朝通好，或派使臣访华，或国王亲率使团访华，甚至郑和没有到过的一些国家如速麻里儿（今索马里）等，也

China or by leading the diplomatic missions to China themselves. Even countries that Zheng He had never been to, Somalia, for instance, sent envoys and kindnesses to China.

Ending his visit to the East Africa, Zheng He's fleet crossed the Indian Ocean, passed by islands like Sumatra and Ceylon and returned to China in early 1423, merely ten months later. He brought with him envoys from 16 countries including Hormuz, a total of 1200 people.

Each of his first few voyages had taken around a year or two, but this one lasted only ten months because he had a mission to complete. He had to escort envoys of 16 countries back home and pick up another 16 who sought to visit China. It was unnecessary to linger in those countries for a long time.

The seventh voyage to the western oceans (1431–1433)

After the first lunar month of 1421, Emperor Yongle moved the capital to Beijing and the former capital, Nanjing, was turned into a vice capital. Three years later, in 1424, Emperor Yongle died. Crown prince Zhu Gaochi succeeded to the throne and changed the name of the era to Hongxi. Knowing nothing about how to run a country, the new emperor lent a ready ear to the slander from Xia Yuanji, the minister of finance, and put an end to the

肯尼亚蒙巴萨的现代博物馆里收藏的当地出土的中国古瓷器
Ancient Chinese porcelain unearthed from local place is kept at the Modern Museum in Mombasa, Kenya.

派使臣到中国访问，带来非洲人民的友谊。

结束了对东非的访问，郑和船队复偕忽鲁谟斯等16国访华使臣1200人横渡印度洋，经锡兰山、苏门答剌等地，于1423年初回到国内，耗时仅十个月。

郑和船队历次下西洋，每次往返需一两年左右，而这次仅用十个月时间，这与他护送16国使臣回国、迎接16国使臣来访的使命有关，没有必要在各国停留很长时间。

第七次下西洋（1431—1433）

1421年正月起，永乐皇帝迁都北京，原来的京师南京成为陪都。三年后（1424年），永乐皇帝病崩，太子朱高炽继位，改年号洪熙。不会治理国家的洪熙皇帝登基后，听信户部尚书夏原吉的谗言，宣布停止下西洋活动。1425年，洪熙皇帝命令郑和带领下西洋的官兵守备南京。洪熙皇帝一年后去世，太子朱瞻基

voyages to the western oceans. In 1425, he ordered Zheng He and his men to guard Nanjing. He died a year later, however. Zhu Zhanji, his son and heir, came into power and changed the name to Xuande. The year 1426 was the first year of the Xuande reign.

During the six years when Zheng He guarded Nanjing, he devoted most of his efforts to supervising the building of the Nanjing Grand Bao'en Temple and its Glazed

The Glazed Pagoda of Nanjing Grand Bao'en Temple

Zheng He built the Glazed Pagoda of Nanjing Grand Bao'en Temple under orders from Emperor Yongle to commemorate his mother. The pagoda was built according to the royal standard and took 100,000 craftsmen and soldiers, 2.48 million liang of silver, and 16 years (1412–1478) to complete.

The pagoda is located on the east side of Yuhua Road, outside the China Gate of Nanjing. It rises up to a height of 80 meters with nine stories in eight directions. The perimeter of the base is about 100 meters. The unique pagoda had stood in Nanjing for more than 400 years (1412–1856) and became a landmark of the city. It iwas known as the "token of Nanjing," "China's great antique" and the "big kiln of Emperor Yongle."

This building was listed as one of the Seven Great Wonders of the Medieval World. Unfortunately, it was almost destroyed during the War of Taiping Heavenly Kingdom (1856). Now the Nanjing government plans to rebuild it on the former site.

继位，年号宣德，1426年为宣德元年。

郑和在南京任守备的六年间，主要精力用于督造南京大报恩寺及琉璃宝塔。雄伟壮观的大报恩寺及琉璃宝塔被誉为"中世纪世界七大奇观"之一。停止下西洋后，西洋各国与中国明朝的关系渐渐疏远，使节

金陵大报恩寺琉璃宝塔

金陵大报恩寺琉璃宝塔，是永乐皇帝为纪念其生母 妃而命郑和主持督建的。宝塔的规格按照皇室图式，使用的匠人和军工达10万人，耗银248万余两，建塔时间长达16年（1412—1478）。

宝塔位于今南京中华门外雨花路东侧，塔高80米左右，九层八面，底层周长约100米，开有四座拱门。整塔白日金碧照耀，夜则灯火腾焰，风铃日夜作响，声闻数里。这座举世无双的琉璃宝塔在金陵土地上屹立400余年之久（1412—1856），为金陵最具特色的地面标志性建筑，曾被人们称为"金陵的表征"、"中国之大古董，永乐之大窑器"，是当时中外人士游历金陵时的必到之处。

这座被中外人士誉之为"中世纪世界七大奇观"之一的金陵大报恩寺琉璃宝塔，惜乎毁于太平天国战争时期（1856年）。今日南京市政府正拟原址重建。

Pagoda. The majestic temple and the glazed pagoda were regarded as one of the seven wonders of the middle ages. The halt of Zheng He's voyages strained relations with western countries. Exchanges of envoys and mutual trade stopped. China's political influence overseas was greatly weakened. To improve the situation, in the sixth lunar month of 1430, Emperor Xuande ordered Zheng He to undertake his seventh voyage to the western oceans.

By this time, Zheng He was already 60 years old. Though his hair was grey, he still held great ambitions and gladly accepted to undertake another voyage to the western oceans. In early 1431, he set off from dragon bay in Nanjing (now Xiaguan) with his fleet and moored in Liujiagang Port in Taicang for a short time. Soon, a great fleet of 60 ships sailed south.

This time, the fleet reached more countries and regions

Seven Great Wonders of the Medieval World

Since the 16th century, people in the west began to learn about the great cultures of the east. They listed seven great wonders of the Medieval world, which include the Great Wall of China, the Glazed Pagoda of Nanjing Grand Bao'en Temple, the Roman Coliseum of Italy, the Underground Vault of Alexandria, Egypt, the Leaning Tower of Pisa, Italy, the Hagia Sophia of Turkey, and Stonehenge in Salisbury, Britain.

往来渐渐中断，对外贸易渐渐萎缩，海外政治影响渐渐削弱。为了改变这一情况，宣德皇帝于1430年农历六月命令郑和第七次下西洋。

此时郑和已年届花甲，虽头发花白，但仍壮心不已，欣然接受第七次下西洋的任务。1431年初，郑和船队从南京龙湾（今下关）出发，先到太仓刘家港暂泊。不久，60多艘海船组成的庞大船队像过去一样从这里启航，扬帆南下。

此次船队所到国家和地区最多，几乎访遍了南洋、北印度洋沿岸地区以及阿拉伯半岛和非洲东岸诸国。最远到达非洲南端接近莫桑比克海峡的某一处。庞大的船队自苏门答剌便开始分头航行，使团分成几个分团同时访问亚非国家。其中一分团由太监洪保率

中世纪世界七大奇观

公元16世纪，西方人开始认识到东方文化的博大精深，将中国的万里长城、金陵大报恩寺琉璃宝塔、意大利罗马大斗兽场、埃及亚历山大地下陵墓、意大利比萨斜塔、土耳其索菲亚大清真寺和英国沙利斯布里石环，并列为中世纪世界七大奇观。

than at any other time. It visited Southeast Asia, banks along the northern Indian ocean, the Arabian peninsula and countries in eastern Africa. The farthest place they reached was southern Africa, near the Mozambique Channel. The fleet was divided into several teams in Sumatra and different delegations visited different countries in Asia and Africa. Eunuch Hong Bao lead one delegation to visit Banggela (now Bangladesh). Banggela had sent multiple envoys loaded with presents to visit China. Among the many presents they sent to China was an auspicious beast kylin (a giraffe). Zheng He's peer, the great scholar Shen Du even painted one picture of the kylin offered by Banggela in 1414, which is still popular today. During Zheng He's voyage to the western oceans, ministers from the Ming Dynasty were especially excited when they saw the giraffe sent by Banggela. Many of them wrote poetry about it and sixteen poetry anthologies were published. When Zheng He's fleet visited Calicut in November 1432, Calicut sent people to Tianfang (which held present-day Mecca) in a pilgrimage. Upon learning of this plan, Zheng He also dispatched seven people, including translator Ma Huan, to accompany them. Tianfang was a cradle of Islam. Every year the country would receive lots of pilgrims. A magnificent mosque that looked like multi-floored pagoda was built using multi-colored stones. The girder and roof were built with

明人画麒麟度颂轴。1414年，长颈鹿首次出现在明朝宫廷中，一度被认为是神兽麒麟。朝野齐声歌颂，视为神圣吉祥物。
Giraffe Painting Eulogized by Shen Du. In 1414, the giraffe firstly appeared in the palace of Ming Dynasty and was regarded as the god animal Kylin. Both the government and the people paid a tribute to Giraffe and regarded it as the holy mascot.

领访问榜葛剌国（今孟加拉）。榜葛剌国曾多次遣使访问中国，赠送许多礼物，其中最引起中国朝野注目的是瑞兽麒麟（长颈鹿）。郑和同时代人、翰林院侍讲学士沈度于1414年绘有《榜葛剌进麒麟图》，流传至今。郑和下西洋期间，明朝文武百官见到海外诸国进献瑞兽麒麟，激动无比，纷纷填词赋诗，后来结集出版诗集《瑞应麒麟诗》达16册之多。

1432年十一月郑和率领的船队访问古里时，正值古里国派人去天方（麦加）朝觐，郑和获知情况后也派通事（翻译）马欢等七人同行。天方国是伊斯兰教大国，又是该教发祥之地，每年从各国各地来此朝圣的伊斯兰教徒很多，十分热闹。这里有雄伟壮丽的清真寺，它像多层大宝塔一样，用各色彩石砌成，以沉香木做梁和顶，大殿里燃着香料，寺内馨香缭绕，虔诚的穆斯林祈祷如仪。天方国街道整齐宽

eaglewood. Spice was lighted in the palace and pious prayers crowded in. The streets in Tianfang were spacious and tidy. Many people from different countries came here to do businesses.

Tianfang is in a semitropical area and is warm throughout all four seasons. People there were very hospitable. Ma Huan and other people of the delegation were well treated. They bought kylins, lions, ostriches and other treasures. They also painted a picture of a paradise, which they brought back. When the delegation left, Tianfang sent envoys with Ma Huan to visit China.

Zheng He's biggest hope was to make a pilgrimage to Tianfang, but unfortunately he was not quite himself at the time and had to give up the idea. It was a great regret for such a man not to be able to realize this dream.

Zheng He's fleet visited Calicut again on the way back home. By then, Zheng He was 62 years old and fell gravely ill due to overwork. At the beginning of the fourth lunar month in 1433, this great navigator who had devoted almost 30 years to his craft, passed away on his gorgeous boat on the sea near Calicut on the west bank of South India. Zheng He, a favorite of the sea, strived at sea, achieved success on the sea and finally passed away on the sea, and found his final resting place at the bottom of the ocean. Because of the death of chief ambassador Zheng He, the fleet cut short the time spent overseas

南京郑和墓，位于牛首山西南麓。
Zheng He's Tomb in Nanjing located in the southwest slope of Niushou Mountain.

敞，市容繁华，世界各地来此经商者很多。

天方国地处亚热带，四时温暖如春，人民淳朴好客。马欢等中国使团人员受到天方国人民的欢迎。他们在当地购得麒麟、狮子、鸵鸟及其他珍宝，还绘制了一张《天堂图》带回来。当使团离开时，天方国派使臣随马欢等人访问中国。

去天方朝觐一直是郑和最大的心愿，但不幸的是此时郑和身体状况欠佳，心有余力而不足了。一代航海英豪未能遂愿赴天方朝觐，后人无不为之感慨。

郑和船队返航途中又到古里。此时，郑和因操劳过度一病不起。这位在海上奋斗近30年的伟大航海

and returned home under the command of another chief ambassador Wang Jinghong, who was a court eunuch. On the way back, some boats of the fleet stopped in Taiwan. Since then, many tales to the eunuch named Sanbao emerged in Taiwan, like Sanbao ginger in Fengshan County of Taiwan. It is said that the Sanbao ginger was brought there by the eunuch name Sanbao and can cure many illnesses. Zheng He's fleet returned to Nanjing during the seventh lunar month of 1433, putting an end to the seventh voyage to the western oceans which lasted for one and a half years.

Zheng He's seven voyages profoundly influenced people in countries along the western oceans. In particular, many people in southeast countries considered the eunuch named Sanbao as a deity.

A huge number of temples were built in Southeast Asian countries to commemorate Zheng He. Many folk fairs were held in each year to honor Zheng He and many myths and legends have raised Zheng He's reputation and spread among people. All of these illustrate the significance of Zheng He's fleet, which visited western oceans and made active and profound influences to Asian countries for a long time.

印尼三宝垄市大觉寺内的三保大人神像（红脸），中间为郑和，两旁是王景弘和马欢。三宝垄是世界上唯一一座为纪念郑和而以他的别称"三保大人"命名的城市。
Statue of Sanbao Monsignor (red face) in Dajue Temple, Semarang, Indonesia. Zheng He is in the middle, and Wang Jinghong and Ma Huan are on both sides. Semarang is the only city named by another name of Zheng He "Sanbao Monsignor" in memory of Zheng He in the world.

家，于1433年农历四月初，在印度南部西海岸卡利卡特附近海上的宝船中病逝，终年62岁。这位海之骄子，奋斗在海上，成功在海上，最终殉职于海上，安息在大海的怀抱之中。

由于正使郑和的逝世，郑和船队便缩短了在海外逗留的时间，由另一正使太监王景弘指挥回航。回航途中，部分船只到台湾作了短暂停留。从此，台湾就有不少关于三保太监的传说，如台湾凤山县有三保姜，相传为三保太监传入，可治多病。郑和船队于1433年农历七月回到南京，从而结束了历时一年半的第七次下西洋的出访活动。

郑和七次出使，在西洋各国人民中留下了深远的影响。尤其东南亚许多国家的人们把三宝太监视为神灵，建庙奉祀，数百年来香火不断，民间流传着有关三宝太监的许多动人故事。马来西亚槟城附近海珠屿

南京郑和纪念馆和郑和塑像
Zheng He Memorial and Zheng He Statue in Nanjing

Monuments, temples and historical sites commemorating Zheng He in countries of Southeast Asia

There are dozens of monuments, temples and historical sites commemorating Zheng He in countries of Southeast Asia, including the statue of Zheng He in Malacca, the Sanbao Well, the Sanbao Mountain, the Sanbao Pavilion, the Sambao Temple in Kuala Lumpur, the Sanbao Cave in Indonesia, the Zheng He mosque and Sanbao Temple in Surabaya, as well as a number of temples in Jakarta, Thailand, Cambodia, and other countries.

的大伯公庙的碑文说："南洋言神，辄称三宝大神，或云三宝即太监郑和也。"郑和在南洋华侨中被尊为"护侨之神"。

东南亚国家建有如此众多的纪念郑和的庙宇，每年举办如此众多的祭祀郑和的民间庙会，流传如此众多的赞颂郑和的神话传说，从一个侧面反映了郑和下西洋对亚非国家产生的积极影响之深之巨之久。

【东南亚各国纪念郑和的寺庙和古迹】

马来西亚马六甲有郑和石像、三宝井、三宝山、宝山亭（即三宝庙）、马六甲博物馆内郑和坐像；吉隆坡有三宝庙，吉隆坡国家博物馆大门上挂有马来西亚历史沿革图第一段（描述1409年郑和船队访问马六甲的热烈场面），槟州有三保宫；沙捞越的古晋有三保宫；印度尼西亚的三宝垄有三保庙、三保洞，三保庙内展有大铁锚（相传是当年郑和船队留下的），三宝垄人民每年农历六月二十九（相传是郑和首次来到三宝垄的日子）抬着大觉寺内供奉的三保大人像（红脸）到三宝洞游行；印尼泗水有三保庙、郑和清真寺；印尼雅加达有三保水厨庙；泰国有三保公庙、三宝塔寺、三宝城、三宝港；柬埔寨磅湛有三保公庙等等。

III

Zheng He's fleet

To fulfill the diplomatic mission entrusted by Emperor Yongle, combat the terrifying waves in the ocean and deal with any possible military action, Zheng He organized the largest fleet of ships the world had ever seen. It featured a great number of sailors, a complete organization, huge size, diverse categories, strict formation and organized communications.

A great number of sailors and complete organization

Zheng's fleet consisted of up to 30,000 sailors. Historical data shows that there were over 27,800 sailors in his first expedition, around 27,000 in the third, 27,670 in the fourth and 27,550 in the seventh. The numbers of sailors in the rest of his seven expeditions was not clearly recorded but estimated to be about 27,000, equaling the combined number of the naval armies of the five "Weis" (a Wei was

3

郑和船队

为圆满完成永乐皇帝交付的下西洋外交航海使命，抗衡大洋上的惊涛骇浪，应付可能出现的军事行动，郑和组建了当时世界上最庞大的大型特混远洋船队。其主要特点是：船员众多，建制完整；船舶巨大，种类齐全；编队严密，通讯便捷。

船员众多，建制完整

郑和船队船员人数近3万之多。据史料记载，第一次为27800余人，第三次为27000余人，第四次为27670人，第七次为27550人。其余几次人数载录不详，但估计也在27000人左右，相当于明初五卫水军之和（每卫5600人）。

船队按所担任务设立五部分编制。它们是：

1.首脑决策：由正使太监、副使监丞、少监、内

a type of military unit with 5,600 sailors) in the early Ming Dynasty.

The fleet included five sub-organizations based on different tasks:

1. Decision-making by fleet heads: The decision-making body consisted of an envoy eunuch and vice-envoy eunuchs of lower positions, who were all ministers of Emperor Yongle and heads of the fleet. Zheng He, as the imperial envoy, was the top leader and commander of the whole fleet. His major assistants included Wang Jinghong, Hou Xian, Li Xing, Hong Bao and Yang Qing.

2. Navigation: The work was executed by such technical personnel as "huozhang," "duogong," "bandingshou," "tiemao," "munian," "dacai," "shuishou," "minshao," "yinyangguan" and "yinyangsheng." The "Huozhang" equaled present-day captains; "Duogong" took charge of steering based on the captain's directions; "Bandingshou" were responsible for anchoring; "Tiemao," "munian" and "dacai" were arranged for all sorts of iron and wood handiwork on board; "Shuishou" and "minshao" were in charge of the sails, oars and other daily chores; and "yinyangguan" and "yinyangsheng" were those who studied and forecast weather conditions.

Foreign trade: Business was handled by officials from "Honglusi" (an organization in the Ming Dynasty established to organize receptions and rituals) as well

2000年发现的《天妃经》卷首插图描绘的郑和下西洋船队。据学者考证，该图为随同郑和第五次下西洋的僧人胜慧刻印。
Zheng He's fleet for the voyages to the west oceans in the photo of the first chapter of the Scripture of Queen of Heaven found in 2000. According to the scholars, the photo was made by Monk Shenghui who accompanied Zheng He in the fifth voyage to the western oceans.

监等组成，均为永乐皇帝的亲信内臣，是船队的指挥中枢。郑和作为钦差正使太监，是船队的最高负责人与指挥者。其主要副手有王景弘以及侯显、李兴、洪保、杨庆等人。

2.航海业务：由火长、舵工、班碇手、铁锚、木舱、捻材、水手、民艄、阴阳官、阴阳生等航海技术人员组成。火长，相当于今日船长；舵工，按火长指令操舵，控制海船航向；班碇手负责起落船锚；铁锚、木舱、捻材负责打制与修理船上各种铁木活计；水手、民稍，负责升帆落篷、摇橹划桨撑篙与日常的清洁保养工作；阴阳官、阴阳生负责天文气象的观测与预报。

as compradors and interpreters. The officials from "Honglusi" were responsible for such diplomatic events as banquets; compradors purchased commodities and interpreters were arranged for language interpretation.

4. Logistics: The work was done by personnel from the Imperial Board of Finance like "langzhong," "sheren," "shusuanshou" and medical officials. "Langzhong" took charge of money and the supply of materials; "Sheren" drafted letters and files; "Shusuanshou" resembled present-day accountants and cashiers; and medical officials treated diseases.

5. Military convoys: The convoy team was composed of armed personnel at various levels including a general commander, commanders, "qianhu," "baihu," "qixiao," "yongshi," "lishi" and "junshi." They were responsible for the safety of navigation, defense against enemies and pirates.

The complete organization of the fleet ensured the successful accomplishment of every task of the voyage and, at the same time, demonstrated the rich experience of ancient Chinese in ocean navigation.

Huge vessels and diverse categories

Zheng He's various expeditions involved over 200 vessels of difference sizes, which indeed constituted a task fleet of fine structure and complete categories.

3.外交贸易：由鸿胪寺序班、买办、通事等组成。鸿胪寺序班负责朝会宴请等外交礼仪；买办负责采购物品；通事负责涉外翻译。

4.总务后勤：由户部郎中、舍人、书算手、医官医士等人员组成。户部郎中负责掌管钱财及后勤供应；舍人负责起草誊写书信文件；书算手负责会计出纳；医官医士负责防治疾病。

5.军事护航：由都指挥、指挥、千户、百户、旗校、勇士、力士、军士等各级武装人员组成，负责航行安全、抵御外敌和海盗。

船队完整的编制，确保了下西洋各项任务的顺利完成，同时展示了明代中国人丰富的远洋航海阅历和经验。

船舶巨大、种类齐全

郑和每次下西洋，出海的大小海船有200余艘，堪称一支结构精良、种类齐全的特混船队。

船队拥有五种船舶类型：宝船、马船、粮船、坐船、战船。

1.宝船：形制大，有九桅，张十二帆。最大宝船

The fleet included five types of ships: Treasure ships, horse ships, grain ships, sitting ships and battle ships.

1. Treasure ship: It was huge with nine masts and 12 sails. The biggest treasure ship was 114m long and 46m wide, which truly was a masterpiece created by the ship makers. China's ship-making sector during the Ming Dynasty was a wonder in the history of wooden sailing ships, reached a peak in ship making by the 19th century and demonstrated the amazing wisdom and talent of the Chinese people in ship making.

2. Horse ship: With eight masts, it was used for both battles and transport.

3. Grain ship: With seven masts, it was designed for grain storage and material supply.

4. Sitting ship: It was also called "battle-sitting ship. " With six masts, it was a place for sailors to rest and camp.

5. Battle ship: With five masts, it was the fast-speed ship for convoys and battles.

In addition, there were also ships to carry a water supply.

Strict formation and easy communications

1. Big ships and small ships: Based on different tasks, the fleet formation could be divided into a "big ship fleet" and a "small ship fleet." The former was responsible for the whole fleet's major tasks, and the latter was in

南京宝船厂遗址6号作塘，有大规模、有规律排列的造船基础遗迹。
No. 6 workshop of Nanjing's Treasure Shipyard, and a large number of archeological findings indicate that this shipyard was indeed where the large-sized ships were built.

长114米，宽46米。建造如此巨大的宝船，堪称明代造船家的杰作。明代中国造船业创造了世界木帆船史上的奇迹，达到了19世纪以前世界木帆船造船业的顶峰。

2.马船：又名马快船，有八桅，作战与运输兼用。

3.粮船：有七桅，用来屯运粮食和后勤供应品。

4.坐船：又名战坐船，有六桅，用来屯存水师和安营扎寨。

5.战船：有五桅，专司护航、作战的快速战船。

此外，还有存储饮用水的水船等。

编队严密，通讯便捷

1.大舻和小舻：船队编列，按任务不同，分为大舻船队和分舻船队。大舻船队完成主要任务，分舻船队负责部分临时任务。两种船队可分可合，机动灵活地完成不同的任务。

charge of some temporary jobs. The two fleets could work together or separately, accomplishing diverse tasks flexibly.

2. Formation: The fleet marched forward in an arrowhead-like formation. The core ships, consisting of the ships with "Shuai"—character flags and treasure ships, were in the center of the fleet, a safe position from where to issue orders and commands. Surrounded by battle ships on every side, the fleet could rapidly change its formation and defend against enemies effectively in case any part was attacked. The horse ships, grain ships and sitting ships that were designed to carry sailors and goods were arranged inside the four sides of the fleet and were protected by battle ships.

The fleet had a convenient communications system to ensure orderly formation and effective dispatching. Flags served as means of communication in the daytime. Every ship was equipped with one big "sitting-flag," one signal strip, 10 mast flags and 50 square-shaped flags. Messages were sent by hanging or waving flags and strips of different colors. Lanterns were used at night, and sound signals would be adopted if bad weather caused poor visibility. Each ship carried gongs and drums of different sizes, which could be used to boost morale in battle and send messages as well. With these convenient communication methods, issuing of such orders such

郑和下西洋仿古宝船
Archaized Treasure Ship for Zheng He's voyages to the western oceans

　　2.编队队形：船队航行时，以箭镞状队形前进。由帅字号船与宝船组成的中军帐，位于船队核心安全部位，便于对各翼发号施令，实施统一的指挥调度。船队前后左右外围，都由战船队列保护，无论哪一翼受到侵扰，均可迅速调整队列，重新形成迎向敌方的编队，以进行有效的抵御。运载人员、货物为主的马船、粮船与坐船，编排在战船四翼的护航圈内，以保障航行安全。

　　为了保证编队整齐，进退有致，实施有效的指挥与调度，船队建立了便捷的通讯联络系统。白天航行以旗帜联络。每船有大坐旗1面、号带1条、大桅旗

as marching forward or backward, dining, resting, assembling, anchoring, sailing or turning-around were made possible.

3. Navigating techniques: Zheng's fleet inherited and carried forward the traditional Chinese techniques of navigating using sails. Monsoons from Southeast Asia, the Northern Indian Ocean and the Arabian Sea regions were the major forces that drove ships forward. As many as 12 sails were used at one time in the large nine-mast ships to maximize the force of the wind. Zheng's fleet further developed wind-driven nautical techniques and could make full use of the wind from all sides. It was those mature techniques that ensured the safe voyage of the fleet in the vast ocean.

Painting and application of *The Map of Zheng He's Navigation*. Navigation maps were one of the most basic and necessary tools for navigation, especially ocean expeditions. *The Map of Zheng He' Navigation* was the earliest picture used for ocean navigation in Chinese history. It has been passed down to this today. It covered a wide area, long navigation courses and recorded numerous names of places. Based on traditional Chinese painting methods, the map, with a scroll roll, stretched out from right to left. It vividly shows dozens of routes that started from the Nanjing Treasure Ship Workshop, through the estuary of the Yangtze River to Fujian and

电脑制作的郑和船队图
Photo of Zheng He's fleet made by PC

10面、正五方旗50面，通过约定方式悬挂或挥舞各色旗带以互通信息。夜晚航行认灯笼。如遇阴雨迷雾天气，海上能见度差，则改以音响信号联络。每船备有大铜锣、小铜锣、大更鼓、小更鼓若干。这些物件除在作战时擂鼓助威、鸣金收兵外，尚可在夜晚或不良天气下传递音响信号。凭藉如此便捷的通讯联络，即可统一指挥船队的前进、后退、举炊、休息、集合、起锚、扯篷、升帆、抛泊、转向等。

3.航海技术：郑和船队继承并发展了中国传统的利用风帆航行的技术，将东南亚、印度洋北部和阿拉伯海季风区的季风作为航行的主要动力。为了最大限度地利用风力，九桅宝船最多时张12帆。船队发展了

郑和航海图 (局部)
Navigation map of Zheng He (part)

Guangdong along China's southwestern coastline via the
Indo-China peninsula. The routes extended westward to
the Indian Ocean through the Malacca Strait and further
to the Arabian Sea and Arabian Peninsula via the Indian
Peninsula, and finally ended in the 10-plus routes along
the coast of East Africa. Geographically speaking, the map
covered a total area that spans from 44 to 122 degrees east
longitude and from 32 degrees north latitude to 8 degrees
south latitude. The water area included the West Pacific
Ocean and the North Indian Ocean. And the land area
spread from Southeast Asia to East Africa and includes
the names of 540 places. The painting of the map was
the result of the application of a combination of multiple

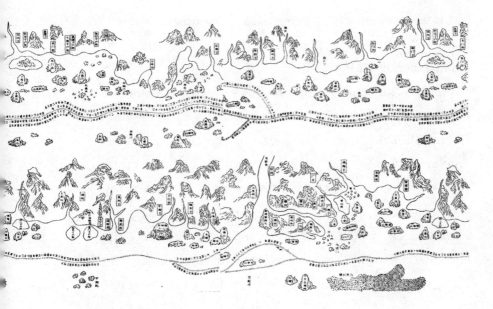

风帆航行技术，能"船行八面风"。正是由于对风帆的使用已驾轻就熟，船队才能随心所欲地纵横驰骋在浩瀚的汪洋大海上。

绘制和应用《郑和航海图》。航海图是航海活动特别是远洋航海活动最基本的也是必不可少的工具之一。《郑和航海图》是中国历史上流传至今的一部最早的远洋航海用图。它涵盖的地域广阔，航线漫长，记录的地名众多。该图运用中国传统绘画手法，写实与写意相结合，以长卷画轴的形式自右向左，形象化地展现以南京宝船厂为起点，出长江口，沿着中国东

nautical techniques like compass navigation, celestial navigation, object navigation, terrestrial navigation and standard navigation speed.

Celestial navigation. Zheng's fleet ingeniously shaped a full set of celestial navigation techniques by combining the traditional Chinese astronomical observation and the "Stellar Technique for Ocean Navigation." When sailing in the ocean, the fleet could be guided by observing coastal objects, the heavenly bodies and the compass. If no objects on land were visible, observation of the sun, the stars and the compass was the basic means for navigation. The "Stellar Technique for Ocean Navigation" served as a method to locate where the ship was in latitude by studying the elevation of the stars in the sky. When using this technique, Zheng's fleet observed more stars that usually involved in both south-north and east-west direction for verification. Those Chinese navigation techniques were far more advanced than those adopted by other countries in the world.

Terrestrial navigation. In this technique, fixed objects on land were used for reference to determine the direction and distance of the trip. It was mainly adopted in offshore voyages. Based on nautical experience, the navigators reminded by surrounding objects, could have a clear picture of the location of potential obstacles, peaks, islands, shoals, reefs, narrow watercourses, as well as the

火长观星图。火长相当于今日船长，他通过观测天体以确证船舶所在方位。
Huozhang's Star Atlas. Huozhang is equivalent to captain today. By observing the celestial body, he can determine the position of ship.

南海岸线直达福建广东，再沿印度支那半岛向西南行，过马六甲海峡向西进入印度洋，再经印度半岛到阿拉伯海和阿拉伯半岛，直到东非沿岸的数十条航路。用今天的地理概念来说，《郑和航海图》的跨度为东经44度至东经122度，北纬32度至南纬8度。就水域来说，包括太平洋西部和印度洋北部；就陆地来说，包括亚洲东南部到非洲东部的广大地区，记录地名多达540多个。它的绘制，是罗盘导航、天文导航、物标导航、地文导航、标准航速（更数）等多种航海技术的综合运用。

天文航海术。郑和船队创造性地继承了古代中国航海观察天象的传统，配合运用"过洋牵星术"，形成了一整套天文航海术。船队在海上航行，一靠对沿岸地形地物的观察，二靠日月星辰的指引，三靠罗盘的导向。在波光接天的海洋中，周围无地物可寻时，"昼则观日，夜则观星，阴晦观指南针"就是船队导

The Stellar Technique for Ocean Navigation

"Ocean navigation" means "traveling through the ocean" and the "stellar technique" was a method used to locate where a ship was in terms of latitude by observing the elevation of the stars in the sky.

Zheng's fleet observed the stars through a special instrument called "stellar plate," which was composed of 12 square plates made of quality wood. The biggest plate was 24cm long. The shortest one was two centimeters long and was called one-thumb plate because it was as long as a thumb. There was another two-inch-long square ivory plate with all of its four corners missing. The lengths of the four missing sides were a half, one eighth, one fourth and three fourths of the side length of the smallest stellar plate, respectively. On the ivory plate were carvings of such characters as "banzhi" (half-thumb), "banjiao" (half-angle), "yijiao" (one-angle) and "sanjiao" (three-angle).

When using the stellar plate, one holds the center of one end of the plate with the left hand, stretches his arms and looks into the sky to make the face of the plate perpendicular to the sea level. One then holds a 60-cm-long string connected to the plate with his right hand. This could help fix the distance between the stellar plate and the eyes of the observer, making the upper edge of the plate visually connected with the stars to be observed and the lower edge visually connected with the line where the ocean meets the sky. Thus, the height of the stars above the sea level could be figured out. During observation, the 12 stellar plates could be alternately used based on the heights of the stars until the fittest is found. The number of "thumbs" of the plate are the height of the star.

The "angle" could be measured through the carvings on the plate or the ivory plate. The principle on which it is based somewhat resembles present-day sextant.

过洋牵星术

"过洋"即"越过海洋"的意思；"牵星术"即通过观测星辰的海平高度（仰角）来确定海上船舶在南北纬度上所处位置的一种方法。

郑和船队牵星术的应用，是通过一种专门用来观测星辰的器具——牵星板来进行的。牵星板是用优质乌木制成的12块正方形木板组成。最大的一块，边长约24厘米；最小的一块，边长2厘米，如一个拇指宽。另有正方形象牙板一块，边长2寸，四角皆缺，缺边长度分别是最小牵星板边长的二分之一、八分之一、四分之一、四分之三。象牙板上刻有半指、半角、一角、三角字样，颠倒相向。

使用牵星板时，左手拿着牵星板一端的中心，手臂伸直，眼看天空，使牵星板板面与海平面垂直，板上引一根长约60厘米的绳子，用右手抓住拉直，以固定牵星板与观测者眼睛之间的距离，使板的上边缘与所测星体相接，下边缘与海天交线相合，这样可得出星体离海平面的高度。观测时，可随星体高度不同，将12块牵星板替换使用，直到选用的那块板上下边缘达到上述要求为止。这时使用的牵星板是几指，这个星体的高度就是这个指数。"角"可以从牵星板上的刻度或用小象牙块量出。其原理相当于现在的六分仪。

depth of water, the symbols of
ports and the correct direction.
Zheng's fleet also employed
other techniques in actual
voyages like measuring the
depth of water through plumb
bobs.

郑和船队指引航向用的罗盘（复制品）
Compass (reproduced) used by Zheng He's fleet

The nautical techniques used by Zheng's fleet were first-class. They helped create the brilliance of the expedition. Regretfully, Zheng's voyages to the Western Ocean haven't been appropriately studied by historians. Most works on world history don't mention Zheng He's seven expeditions or their geographical discoveries. That is quite unfair. Despite the bigger influence of the great geographical discoveries on world history, the nautical techniques Zheng's fleet employed went far beyond those adopted by European navigators, so did the nautical accomplishments it achieved.

牵星板模型
Model of Star-aligning Board

航的三种基本方法。郑和船队使用牵星术时，使用的星辰较多，并且常常是南北或东西两星同时并用，互相核正。这些导航技术超过了当时世界其他国家的天文导航水平。

地文航海术。地文航海术主要以陆地上固定的目标作为参照物或陆标，来确定航行的方向和距离。它属于近海航行时所使用的方法。由于航海经验的积累，船队实际航行时，对航行途中的碍航物、山峰、岛屿、浅滩、礁石、险狭水道、水深、底质、港口标志以及正确的定位与航向，均有明确的提示。郑和船队在实际航行中，还运用了其他技术，如用铅锤测量水深等。

郑和下西洋所应用的航海技术，在当时是世界一流的。它成就了世界航海探险的辉煌。然而令人遗憾的是，多少年来，在世界历史的研究中，郑和下西洋并没有得到应有的评价，许多世界通史著作的地理大发现部分没有提到中国郑和的七下西洋。这是不公正的。地理大发现虽然在世界历史上的客观影响大于郑和下西洋，然而郑和下西洋的航海水平及航海成就却远远超过了欧洲航海家。

IV

Sino-foreign cultural exchanges on an unprecedented scale

Zheng He's world-famous expeditions to the Western Ocean was actually a great Sino-foreign cultural exchange on an unprecedented scale when viewed from a cultural perspective. At that time, most Asian and African countries were less developed both economically and culturally when compared to China in the Ming Dynasty. As a result, the relatively advanced Chinese culture was bound to flow into the relatively backward Asian and African countries, as is described in the principle of Cultural Communication, which says one culture, based on its actual needs, will always absorb something else from another culture that it doesn't own. The big cultural exchange initiated by Zheng He was mainly reflected in three aspects: Material cultural exchange, spiritual cultural exchange and institutional cultural exchange.

4

规模空前的中外文化交流

15世纪初声振中外的郑和下西洋，如以文化交流这一视角来审视，不啻是一次规模空前的中外文化大交流。当年，许多亚非国家与明代中国相比，还处在较为后进的社会发展阶段，其文化相对落后于中国文化。由于文化势差和"互通有无"法则的存在，一方文化总是根据自己的需要吸纳另一方文化中自己所不曾有的东西；相对先进的中国文化必然流向相对后进的亚非国家。这次文化大交流，主要在物质文化、精神文化和制度文化三个层面上展开。

物质文化的交流

郑和七下西洋，主要通过赏赐、贸易、朝贡等途径，与亚非国家展开物质文化的交流。郑和船队经由海路输向亚非国家的物品，计有瓷器、丝绸、茶叶、

Material cultural exchange

Zheng's fleet carried out material cultural exchanges with Asian and African countries primarily through largess, trade and tributes. The goods they exported to alien countries included porcelains, silk, tealeaves, lacquers, copper coins, iron farm tools and metalwork.

Porcelains, as one of the greatest inventions of the Chinese people, were a significant contribution made in the history of human culture. The Chinese blue and white porcelains produced during the Ming Dynasty were exported by Zheng's fleet as presents and commodities to Asian and African countries via sea routes. Before Zheng He's expedition, the people in some Asian and African countries had no food containers and had to use the leaves or shells of certain tropical plants instead, but after Zheng's expedition, Chinese porcelains gradually emerged among Asian and African people and further changed their way of life and enriched their material culture. It was for this reason that the maritime route Zheng's fleet opened to connect China with other Asian and African countries became known as the "Road of Porcelain."

Zheng introduced lots of Chinese silk products to Asian and African countries and other areas through largess, trade and tribute. Silk products during the Ming Dynasty mainly included silk scarves, laces, gauze, patterned

明代青花桃竹纹梅瓶和牵牛花纹鸡心碗
Vase with Underglaze Blue and Peach and Bamboo Partners and Lien-tzu Bowl with Morning Glory Patterns

　　漆器、铜钱、铁制农具、金属制品等，以瓷器、丝绸为大宗。

　　瓷器作为中华民族的伟大发明之一，对人类文化的发展作出了卓越的贡献。明初盛产的中国青花瓷器，被郑和船队选作主要礼品和商品整船整船地经由海路向亚非国家输出。郑和下西洋前，有些亚非国家人民饮食无器皿，只能因陋就简地利用热带植物的茎叶或果壳作为饮食器皿；郑和下西洋后，以青花瓷为代表的中国瓷器逐渐成为亚非人民普遍使用的饮食器

fine silk, embroidered fine silk, golden silk clothes with embroidered dragons, golden veiling and baldachins. Those exquisitely-made Chinese silk products were deeply loved by both officials and civilians in Asia and Africa. It was Zheng He's voyage that made the Asian and African people in the middle ages enjoy advanced silk civilization and affected by the Chinese silk culture in such respects as silk weaving and garment making.

Huge foreign demand for Chinese silk products in return promoted the development of the domestic silk industry. During the early Ming Dynasty, officially-funded weaving bureaus with jurisdiction over the silk industry emerged and quickly sprung up like mushrooms all over the country. Besides Nanjing, other cities like Hangzhou, Shaoxing, Jinhua, Ningbo, Suzhou, Zhenjiang, Chengdu and Jinan all saw the establishment of silk-weaving bureaus that organized silk production and export.

The tea culture was another great invention of the Chinese people and a brilliant pearl the Chinese nation contributed to the human cultural treasury. When Zheng He's fleet visited Siam, they distributed tea seeds to local farmers and this gave rise to a tea-drinking fashion that swept over Siam and the rest of the Indo-China Peninsula. This is why the pronunciation of "tea" in Thai is the same as that in Chinese.

Siamese used to eat the mineral salt exploited from

皿，从而改变了他们的生活习俗，提高了他们饮食文化的层次，丰富了他们的物质生活。有鉴于此，郑和下西洋所开辟的中国联系亚非国家之间的海上之路，也被誉为"陶瓷之路"。

郑和下西洋，通过赏赐、贸易、朝贡回赠等方式，将大量中国丝绸产品传播到亚非国家和地区。明代中国丝绸产品主要有丝巾、冠带、纱罗、锦绮、文绮、织金文绮、蟒龙金织衣、销金帐幔、黄盖、华盖等。这些精美的中国丝绸产品，深受亚非各国官民的喜爱。中世纪亚非各国人民正是通过郑和下西洋丝绸制品的外传，享受到先进的中国丝绸文明，并在丝织技术、服饰文化等方面受到中国丝绸文化的影响。

郑和下西洋对外销丝绸产品的大量需求，反过来促进了国内丝织业的发展。明初，管辖丝绸行业的官办织造局应运而生，且遍及全国。除京师南京外，杭州、绍兴、金华、宁波、苏州、镇江、成都、济南等地，均开设织造局，组织丝绸生产和外销。

茶文化是中华民族的一项伟大创造，是中华民族贡献给人类文化宝库的一件瑰宝。郑和船队到暹罗访问时，曾将中国茶籽分配给暹罗农民种植推广，使饮

remote mountains. But the lack of iodine in the salt resulted in swelling thyroid glands. After his arrival, Zheng He helped them make sea salt and told them that sea salt can also help dispel heat and remove toxic substances. This made local people quite pleased because many of them tended to catch skin lesions due to the hot weather. Besides, Zheng He also taught the Siamese how to cut wood, make porcelain, dig wells and reclaim terraces, which greatly boosted local productivity.

Chinese fishing nets were introduced into Cochin, India through Zheng's voyage. Unfortunately, Zheng He died of disease when passing by Calicut during his seventh voyage. After his death, some of his attendants were left to keep vigil and later moved to Cochin, south of Calicut, because of flood. They brought Chinese fishing nets there. The fishing nets, based on the principle of leverage, have four corners tied on four long wooden sticks, the tops of which join together and are fixed to a strong long pole. The pole is further supported by a very high bracket. Taking a net out of the water surface required the joint efforts of five or six fishermen. Fishermen would take out the nets while singing a work song, then the fishing net would slowly rise out of the surface accompanied by the creaks of the poles, leaving fish thrashing about at the bottom of the net. At that time, one of the fishermen would walk closer with a tuck net and catch fish from the

茶之风传遍暹罗及中南半岛国家。泰语中的"茶"与汉语中的"茶"发音一样。

　　暹罗人习惯吃深山里开采的矿盐，矿盐缺碘，致使不少暹罗人甲状腺肿大。郑和去后，帮助他们制造海盐，并告诉他们海盐盐水还有消火败毒之功效。该国气候酷热，生疮患疖的人特别多，懂得这个常识后，人们欣喜万分，无不感激郑和。此外，郑和还派人向暹罗人传授伐木、烧制陶器、凿井、开垦梯田等先进技术，促进了暹罗社会生产力的提高。

　　中国渔网由郑和船队传入印度科钦。郑和船队第七次下西洋返航至古里时，郑和不幸病逝。郑和在古里病逝后，留下一些侍从守灵，后来由于洪水泛滥，这些中国人迁往南边的科钦，并将中国渔网带到这里。渔网利用杠杆原理，将四角系在四根长木上，四根长木的顶端收拢在一起，被固定在一根粗大的长杆上。长杆

中国渔网不仅是科钦的传统渔具，也是吸引游客的重要旅游资源。
Chinese fishing net is not only the traditional fishing tool at Kochin, but also an important tourism resource that attracts tourists.

big net. They could once again drop the fishing net back into the water and withdraw it more than ten minutes later. Before the introduction of Chinese fishing nets, people in Cochin had caught fish sitting on canoes, which proved to be very inefficient. The application of Chinese fishing nets not only greatly improved productivity, but also saved labor and reduced the risks of sea fishing. Surprisingly, the Chinese fishing nets are still widely used today. Nowadays, the sculpture of Chinese fishing net erected on the beach beside the estuary of Cochin has become a symbol of the city and a major tourist attraction.

Located in semi-tropical regions, the Champa Kingdom had fertile land and plenty of rain, which was quite suitable for paddy rice planting. Local farmers there, however, used to grow paddy rice only once a year. Zheng He then sent someone to teach them how to improve the planting methods and help them plant paddy rice three times a year, which proved a success. In addition, local people were also taught to dig wells, take water for irrigation, build terraces on mountainsides and use Chinese ploughs that were given them as a present. Ever since then, Champa Kingdom has grown famous for producing paddy rice and the people there gradually led a well-off life. In Malacca, the roofs of houses were made of coconut leaves and canes. The house was not divided into functional sections for dining, cooking or

用很高的支架支起。将浸在水中的一张渔网吊出水面，需五六个渔民操作。渔民们在整齐的号子声中拉动绳索起网，渔网在长木咯咯吱吱的声响中缓慢升出水面，留在网上的鱼儿就在网底蹦跳。此时，一个人操长竿网兜上前，将鱼兜进网兜，就抓到了活鱼。然后再把网放入水中，十几分钟后再起第二网。在中国渔网传入之前，科钦人一直采用坐独木舟叉鱼的方式捕鱼，生产效率极低。而用中国渔网，不仅极大地提高了生产效率，还节省了人力和降低了出海的风险。中国渔网经600多年的风雨，至今盛行不衰。现在科钦入海口的海滩上，那高高矗立在海边的中国渔网成了科钦标志性的景物和推广旅游的名片。

占城国地处亚热带，土地肥沃，雨量充沛，适宜水稻种植。然而占城农民习惯一年种一季稻。郑和派人教农民改进耕作技术，试种一年三季稻，获得成功。此外还教他们凿井，取水灌溉，沿山腰修建梯田，赠送中国犁，教授使犁方法。从此，占城就以生产稻米出名，逐步富庶起来。满剌加国盖房用椰树叶覆盖，用细藤条捆扎以作房顶，一家人寝食厨厕都在一处，晚间不分男女睡一起。郑和派人教满剌加人建

sleeping, and the whole family slept together regardless of gender. Zheng He dispatched his fellows to teach them how to build houses and transported tiles there from China to make roofs. The local people were also told how to plant Chinese herbs to treat diseases. Many of the medicinal materials currently used in Southeast Asia were introduced from China during Zheng's voyage.

Such countries as Calicut, Cochin, Kollam and Quilon suffered from hot weather and summer diseases at that time. The doctors on Zheng's fleet actively treated patients with the medicine they carried, which, however, was not enough anyway. Then, the Chinese doctors used the Chinese skin scraping methods, which proved rather effective and substituted part of the medicine. Since then, the traditional Chinese therapy has gained popularity among the Indian Peninsula.

Cotton had never been planted in such East African countries like Mogadiscio, Brava and Juba. After his arrival, Zheng He found the soil there was very suitable for cotton planting. He gave local residents Chinese seeds and taught them to plant cotton, which proved quite effective. Africans who had never grown cotton, of course, didn't have knowledge of spinning. Zheng He taught them how to spin threads out of cotton and how to make simple looms by binding wood sticks into a bracket. Local women learnt to use shuttles and weave cotton cloth.

造房屋，并从中国带去砖瓦给他们盖顶，还派船队医生教他们种植中草药材，用中药治病防病。至今东南亚有不少药材就是郑和下西洋时从中国带去种植的。

古里、柯枝、大葛兰、小葛兰等国，天气炎热，暑病流行。郑和船队的医生主动给这些国家的暑病患者治病，然而患者多，带去的痧药总不够用。于是船队医生采用中国"刮痧"方法引病外出，收到疗效，克服了少药的困难。自此，这种方法风行印度半岛。

木骨都刺、卜刺哇、竹步等东非国家向来不种棉花。郑和去后，看到那里的土壤适宜植棉，就把中国棉籽送给当地居民教他们种植，效果不错。从不种植棉花的这些国家的人民自然不懂纺织技术。郑和教他们用手抽花成线，又指导他们用木棍扎成一个木架，做成原始简陋的织布机。当地妇女终于学会跪地用手穿梭，织成棉布。从此，这些国家有了自制的棉布，改进了服饰，提高了生活质量。

西洋物产丰富，若干物货为中国人民日常生活所不可缺。东南亚盛产的香料不仅种类齐全，而且量多质优。多种香药的发现和利用，是东南亚人民对世界文明所作的贡献之一。这些香料，实乃中国不可缺者。因

Since then, the people in those African countries have led a better life with cotton cloth and nicer clothes.

The places where Zheng's fleet reached also had abundant products, many of which were daily necessities in China. For instance, the spices produced in Southeast Asia were diverse but of high quality. The discovery and use of a wide range of spices was really a great contribution by the people of Southeast Asia to world civilization. Given the importance of spices, Emperor Yongle sent Zheng He to buy spices in large quantities and bring them to China.

Trade of fragrant medicines between China and Southeast Asia had long existed prior to Zheng He's voyages. Imported fragrant medicines were luxuries exclusive to the rich and inaccessible to common people. But Zheng He's voyages changed that pattern by pushing the trade in fragrant medicines to its height, which further enriched China's food culture. For example, peppers, a result of the ocean trade initiated by Zheng He, were sold everywhere in the Chinese market and even used as a substitute for coins. These peppers, which became cheaper and cheaper, turned into daily necessities rather than precious goods.

The bird's nest that Zheng's fleet brought back from Southeast Asia enriched traditional Chinese herbs and Chinese food culture. It has been noted that the sailors

此，永乐皇帝命郑和大量购买奇香异药以补所缺。

郑和下西洋之前，中国与东南亚的香药贸易早已存在，所得香药属富贵人家的奢侈品，寻常百姓家并不普及。郑和下西洋将香药贸易推向高峰，使香料得以与百姓日常生活联系起来，丰富了中华民族的饮食文化。以胡椒为例，郑和远洋贸易的结果，使胡椒大量充斥中国市场，甚至成为货币的代用品，与宝钞、绢布相互替用。价格一降再降的胡椒，由珍品变为日常用品。

郑和船队从东南亚带回的燕窝，丰富了中药材宝库和中国饮食文化。据载，郑和船队在婆罗洲北岸停泊时，船员曾登陆向当地居民学会采集燕窝做汤喝，以调剂船员的伙食营养。船队归国后，将东南亚产的燕窝献给永乐皇帝享用，得到永乐皇帝的赞赏。从此，燕窝风靡中国。与此同时，郑和船队为亚非国家带去中国生产的人参、麝香、大黄、肉桂、茯苓、姜等中药材，丰富了西洋本土药物。

郑和船队引进的珍稀动植物还有：麒麟（长颈鹿）、狮子、西府海棠、詹匐花、五谷树、娑罗树、龙涎香、沉香、黄熟香、返魂香等，增长了中国人的

of the fleet, when reaching the northern bank of Borneo, learned to make bird's nest soup from local people to improve their diet. Upon their return, they presented the bird's nest produced in Southeast Asia to Emperor Yongle, who spoke highly of it. Bird's nest soon gained popularity across China. Meanwhile, the Chinese herbs taken by Zheng's fleet to Asian and African countries, including ginseng, muskiness, rhubarb, cinnamon, Tuckahoe and ginger, diversified local varieties.

Rare animals and plants Zheng He's fleet introduced to China also included kylins (giraffes), lions, midget crabapple, fontanesia forrunei, Sal tree, ambergris, eaglewood, Aloeswood and senecio cannabifolius. This increased knowledge in China and enriched Chinese animal and plant species.

The fontanesia forrunei (or "five-grain tree" in Chinese) brought back by Zheng He was known as the "sacred tree." Both the Bao'en Temple and Tianjie Temple in Nanjing had one. It got its name from its fruit that resembles five kinds of grains—paddy rice, wheat, soy bean, corn and broomcorn—in shape. It was said that the "five-grain tree" could portend the crop harvest of the next year. Farmers would stand under the tree and watch the fruits carefully every time as the spring sowing approached. The grain that the greatest number of the fruits in the tree resembled would be planted that year.

见识，丰富了中国动植物学科。

郑和从西洋引进的五谷树，被誉为"神树"。南京报恩寺和天界寺各栽有一株。由于其树结子状如稻、麦、黄豆、玉米、高粱五种谷物，故名五谷树。相传此树可预兆来年庄稼的丰歉。农民在每年春播前到五谷树下观察，见树上结的果实像哪一种谷物的居多，当年就播种这种谷物。目前此树已分布在中国的江

印尼井里汶的郑和船队铁锚
Anchor of Zheng He's fleet at Cirebon in Indonesia.

苏、浙江、山东、河南等地。

郑和船队还引进了玻璃制造术。据史料记载："明时三宝太监出洋携带烧玻璃二人来中国。"这是中国传入玻璃制造术、自己烧制玻璃的开始。

中国书籍是中国文化的物质载体之一。郑和使团将中国书籍赠送亚非国家，目的是宣扬中国传统文化，倡导"以和为贵"、"和衷共济"、"和睦相处"、"共享太平"的理念。郑和访问暹罗时，曾赠送《古今列女传》100本，目的是让当地人以中国列女

The trees have now been widely distributed in such areas as Jiangsu, Zhejiang, Shandong and Henan.

Zheng He's fleet also introduced glass-making techniques. Zheng Zi Tong, written by Zhang Zilie of the Ming Dynasty said, "Eunuch Sanbao of the Ming Dynasty, after sailing to the Western Oceans, brought back two technicians who could burn glass." That was the beginning of glass-burning in China. Glass had been considered precious until the middle Ming Dynasty, underscoring Zheng He's great contributions to China's glass industry.

Chinese books are among the material carriers of Chinese culture. Zheng's fleet gave Chinese books to other Asian and African countries as gifts, with a view to spreading traditional Chinese culture and advocating such concepts long cherished by the Chinese people as "peace is valued," "working together with one heart in times of difficulty," "living in harmony" and "sharing common peace." When visiting Siam, Zheng He once donated 100 *"Legendaries of Heroic Chinese Women"* to the local people, in a bid to teach them about the heroines, honor, clemency and peace, and become more dutiful, more enlightened and less aggressive. During Zheng He's voyages, many envoys to China requested the imperial government to give them Chinese books and agreed to exchange them for their local products. The kingdoms of Champa, Java

为楷模，改变叛服无常、喜战好斗的野蛮习性，提高文明开化程度。郑和下西洋期间，不少访华使臣主动要求明朝政府赠给他们中国书籍，并表示愿以本国土特产品来交换。占城、爪哇、暹罗等国拥有丰富的中国书籍，国王及大臣常用中国书籍供子女学习。占城国王还下令设国子院，招年轻学子入院学习，讲授中国四书五经。

精神文化上的交流

伊斯兰教的传播是东南亚历史上最重要的事件之一。郑和下西洋对伊斯兰教在东南亚的传播起了巨大的推动作用。

郑和每次在爪哇等地停留期间，都积极地从事传播伊斯兰教的活动。1405年郑和访问爪哇后，1407年在旧港便产生了华人伊斯兰教区。1411年，在雅加达地区的安卓尔、井里汶、杜板、锦石、若班及爪哇，先后建立清真寺。1413年，当郑和船队停泊在三宝垄时，郑和与他的随从人员马欢、费信一起去当地的清真寺祈祷。至1430年，郑和已成功地在爪哇奠下伊斯兰教信奉的基础。郑和先后在爪哇、旧港、山巴斯

and Siam had a great number of Chinese books, which the kings and ministers often used to teach their children. The king of Champa even ordered an institute of traditional Chinese culture be set up to instruct youths about *The Four Books* (*The Great Learning, The Doctrine of the Mean, The Confucian Analects, and The Works of Mencius*) and *The Five Classics* (*The Book of Songs, The Book of History, The Book of Changes, The Book of Rites, and The Spring and Autumn Annals*).

Spiritual cultural exchanges

The spread of Islam was one of the most significant events in the history of Southeast Asia. Zheng He's voyages played a very big role in helping spread Islam in Southeast Asia. In every one of his stays in such areas as Java, he would vigorously join in the spread of Islam. Following Zheng's visit to Java in 1405, Chinese Islamic parishes appeared in the Old Port in 1407. Mosques were successively built in Andro, Cirebon, Tuban, Gresik, Ruoban and Java in Jakarta in 1411. In 1413 when Zheng's fleet stopped at Semarang, Zheng He and his attendants, Ma Huan and Fei Xin, went together to the local mosque to pray. By 1430, Zheng He had laid a sound foundation in Java for the embrace of Islam. He advocated Islam in Chinese in Java, the Old Port and Kalimantan Barat, and established Chinese Muslim communities as well, which

马六甲三宝山下的宝山亭（郑和庙），建庙工匠、材料均来自中国福建。
Baoshan Pavilion (Zheng He Temple) at the foot of Mt. Sanbao in Malacca. Both the craftsmen and materials used in construction of the temple came from Fujian, China.

（西加里曼丹）用汉语宣扬伊斯兰教，建立穆斯林华人社区，为伊斯兰教在印尼的传播作出了贡献。

郑和支持满刺加发展成为一个强大的伊斯兰王国。1409年，郑和奉命册封拜里迷苏刺为满刺加国国王，赐予银印、冠带、袍服，力挺满刺加发展为强大的国家。满刺加的强大给该国的改宗注入真正的动力，使之一跃成为东南亚重要的商业中心和伊斯兰教的传播中心。

印度尼西亚和马来西亚两国伊斯兰教的传播和发展，郑和功不可没。从这个意义上说，郑和堪称联接

played a big role in spreading Islam in Indonesia.

Zheng He greatly supported Malacca to become a strong Islamic kingdom. In 1409, the Chinese emperor entrusted Zheng He to confer the title of King of Malacca on Jayaviravarman, awarding him the silvery seal, crowns and robes. The growth of the nation gave impetus to its proselytism, which made it an important commercial center and a center for Islam in Southeast Asia.

Zheng He made an immense contribution to the spread and development of Islam in Indonesia and Malaysia. In this sense, Zheng He can be reputed as a navigator who connected China with the Muslim world.

Zheng He was a pious Muslim and Buddhist. He was so versatile that he even knew the art of Buddhist architecture. On one hand, Zheng He introduced traditional Chinese architecture into Southeast Asia, helping Siam build the Pagoda of Three Treasures, the Temple for Rituals, the West Tower and Ximen; He also studied the local art of Buddhist architecture and visited Angkor Wat in Kmir to prepare for the construction of the Grand Bao'en Temple in Nanjing. And the Nanjing Grand Bao'en Temple, which Zheng He built after his return, was indeed a spectacle with proper application of the cultural elements typical of Southeast Asian Buddhist architecture. Widely acknowledged by visitors both at home and abroad, it has been listed among the world's

南京静海寺，为明政府嘉奖郑和功勋而建，郑和曾在此居住。寺内主要供奉郑和从海外带回来的珍宝，有水陆罗汉画像、佛乐等。院内种植有西府海棠等树。
Jinghai Temple in Nanjing constructed by the Government of Ming Dynasty as a commendation to Zheng He's merit. Zheng He once lived in the temple. In the temple, treasures brought by Zheng He from overseas countries were worshiped in the temple, such as figure of amphibus arhat and Buddhist music. Chaenomeles sinensis are planted in the yard.

中国与伊斯兰世界的航海家。

郑和既是一位虔诚的穆斯林，也是位虔诚的佛教徒。他具有多方面的才能，深谙佛教建筑艺术。他一方面把中国的建筑艺术传到东南亚，帮助暹罗建造三宝寺塔、礼拜寺、西塔和锡门，一方面研习东南亚的佛教建筑艺术，考察真腊的吴哥古寺，为在南京建造大报恩寺塔准备条件。由郑和建造的南京大报恩寺塔，吸收了东南亚佛教建筑文化元素，雄伟壮观，受到中外人士普遍赞扬，认为是可与意大利罗马大斗兽

seven great mediaeval wonders that also include the Roman Coliseum of Italy, the Leaning Tower of Pisa, Italy and the underground vault of Alexandria, Egypt. Zheng He moved two Buddhist tile pagodas from Southeast Asia to somewhere in front of the Xuefeng Temple (also called Chongsheng Temple), located at the southern foot of the Phoenix Mountain in Minhou County, Fujian Province. Today, the sites are still there despite the fall of the pagodas. Zheng He made great efforts to boost the spread of Buddhist culture between China and Southeast Asia.

Zheng He also carried back Buddhist paintings with alien features. The portrait of an amphibious arhat hung in the Jinghai Temple, Nanjing, was a piece of premium artwork Zheng He brought back for public display. Yu Chan of the Ming Dynasty said "the portrait of the arhat incorporates superb workmanship excelling nature" and "everybody, old or young, men and women, rush to have a look."

Some Asian and African countries Zheng visited boasted wonderful carving art. The places where the kings lived were decorated with exquisitely-carved hardwood patterns of flowers and beasts. The stone carvings in Angkor Wat, which is part of the world's artistic treasures, include bas-reliefs, high reliefs and full reliefs. The carvings inside the cloisters of Angkor Wat are bas reliefs that describe mythical stories and scenes from daily life.

场、意大利比萨斜塔和埃及亚历山大地下陵墓等相媲美的中世纪世界七大奇观之一。郑和还把东南亚的两座佛教瓦塔，移置福建闽侯县凤凰山南麓的雪峰寺（又名崇圣寺）前。如今塔已早废，遗址尚在。郑和为中国与东南亚的佛教文化交流作出了努力。

郑和注意亚非国家富有民族特色的佛教绘画，热心介绍到中国来。南京静海寺张挂的水陆罗汉像，便是郑和从西洋带回来公开让百姓参观的海外绘画精品。明人俞产赞道："阿罗汉像，水陆毕陈，巧夺造化之奇"，"都人士女，竞相观之"。

郑和所访问的有些亚非国家的雕刻艺术相当精美。榜葛剌等国国王的住所，都用硬木雕刻花鸟兽状，极其精巧。吴哥古迹的石雕艺术，属世界珍品，分浅浮雕、深浮雕和圆雕三大类。吴哥寺回廊上用来表

福建莆田湄洲岛上的天妃立塑石像
Stone statue of the Queen of Heaven at Meizhou Island, Putian, Fujian

Those decorated on ceilings and stone columns are deep reliefs of flowers, trees, birds and beasts. Most carvings of Buddha are full reliefs. With smooth lines and vivid shapes, the carvings were introduced by Zheng's team to China. It was recorded that the lively patterns of lions, dragons, fish, shrimps and sea beasts carved on the white stone "Flying-Rainbow Bridge" that was once located behind the Guangzhi Palace (the southern exit of todays' Nanchizi, in the eastern part of the Golden River in front of Tian'anmen Square, Beijing), west of Huangshicheng (the royal archives of the Ming Dynasty), in the Ming Dynasty were brought back by Zheng He from overseas. In addition, a Buddhist monk named "Fei Huan" who went along with Zheng He in his voyage carried back a statue of arhat carved out of eaglewood, which had a positive influence upon Chinese Buddhist art.

Zheng's voyages to the Western Oceans also pushed forward the spread of Mazu culture, a branch of Chinese Taoism. Mazu (also called the Queen of Heaven) was the goddess of navigation and respected by the people in China's southeastern coastal areas. Many of the 20,000 sailors in Zheng's fleet adored Mazu. As the leader of the fleet, Zheng He naturally turned to supernatural powers for blessings and regarded it as mental support for the whole crew. Zheng He was so pious that every time he set off he would pray to Mazu for safety and when he came

现众多人物的神话故事及生活场景，属于浅浮雕；天花板和石柱上装饰的花木鸟兽等图案，属于深浮雕；其中诸多佛像的雕刻，多属圆雕。这些雕刻，线条流畅，栩栩如生，立体感强。郑和使团把它吸收过来，传入中国。据载，明代北京皇史宬（专藏皇帝手笔、实录、秘典的藏书处）以西正中广智殿后（今北京天安门金水河东段南池子南口）曾有一座飞虹桥，用白石砌成，石上雕刻有狮、龙、鱼、虾、海兽，水波汹涌，活泼如生。这些石雕就是郑和从西洋带回国内的。另外，一位随郑和出使的非幻禅师从西洋带回的

湄洲岛天妃宫里表现妈祖保佑郑和船队平安的壁画
Fresco describing Matsu's bless of safety of Zheng He's fleet in the Palace of the Queen of Heaven at Meizhou Island

back he would thank her for her blessings. Zheng He had Mazu palaces and Tianfei temples built in many places like Nanjing, Taicang, Changle and Meizhouyu, and had the temples repaired more than once. He also established tablets on which the merits of Mazu were recorded. The inscriptions, carved on the "Tablet on the Magic Power

Matsu

Matsu (also called the Empress of Heaven or the Queen of Heaven) is the goddess of navigation worshiped by people in coastal areas in the southeast of China. In ancient times, ocean navigation was often impacted by winds and waves and thus resulted in vessel sinking and death. Safety of seamen became the biggest headache of voyagers, who thus placed hopes on protection of gods. Sacrifice will be offered to the Queen of Heaven before the navigation to pray for downwind and safety. A tablet of the Queen of Heaven was also placed and worshiped on the vessel.

Matsu has been regarded as the goddess of navigation for more than 1,000 years from the Song, Yuan, Ming and Qing dynasties. In recent few years, the culture of Matsu was also spread worldwide with the footprints of Chinese. So far, the total number of the Palace of Matsu reaches over 5,000, and the number of Matsu disciples totals 250 million. Matsu has become the common belief of 90 percent of overseas Chinese. The belief of Matsu has become a network system covering most countries worldwide and functioning as the community center of overseas Chinese.

一堂罗汉像，系用沉香木雕刻而成，"像最奇古，香更异常"，对中国佛教艺术产生了积极影响。

　　郑和下西洋促进了属于中国道教门类的妈祖文化向域外的传播。随郑和下西洋的2万多名船员中，不少人崇拜妈祖。作为船队的统帅，郑和顺其自然，把航海平安的希望投向超自然力的神力，将妈祖奉为全体航海人员精神上的寄托。郑和对妈祖的崇拜十分虔诚，祭礼活动极为频繁。每次出发下西洋前，均隆重祭拜妈祖，以

妈祖

　　妈祖（又称天妃、天后）是中国东南沿海人民广为崇信的航海女神。古代，海上航行经常受到风浪的袭击而导致船沉人亡，船员的安全成为航海者的主要问题，他们把希望寄托于神灵的保佑。在船舶启航前要先祭天妃，祈求保佑顺风和安全，在船舶上还立天妃神位供奉。

　　妈祖作为护航海神，自宋经元、明、清等几代传播，迄今已历千年以上。近代以来，妈祖文化也随着华人的足迹遍及全球。目前全世界的妈祖宫达5000多家，妈祖信徒达2.5亿人。妈祖成了90%的海外华人的共同信仰。妈祖信仰成了一个能横跨世界大多数国度又同时都作为华侨社区中心的网络体系。

of Tianfei" that was launched by Zheng He in Changle County, Fujian, were all about the gratitude he showed to the goddess.

The Mazu worship that began from the early Song Dynasty in the coastal areas of Fujian developed through Zheng's voyage to the Western Oceans. As more and more Chinese people moved to Southeast Asia ("Xia Nan Yang" in Chinese), the worship spread to Southeast Asia and further to European and American countries. Nowadays, there are about 2,500 Mazu temples throughout the world, with over 100 million Mazu followers. Mazu culture has developed into a Chinese folk culture that is widely embraced by the offspring of Yandi and Huangdi.

Institutional cultural exchange

A "Celestial Empire courtesy system," with the Chinese feudal dynasties as the center, had long existed in the east prior to western colonial invasion. Zheng He earnestly executed the decrees of Emperor Yongle to maintain his Celestial Empire courtesy system during his seven voyages. He visited more than 30 countries and regions in Asia and Africa and consistently carried out the policy of "peaceful diplomacy," convincing others by truths and educating others by morality. This helped reinforce the Celestial Empire courtesy system dominated by China of the Ming Dynasty and create the amazing spectacle

祈求远航平安；归航后，又隆重祭祀妈祖，以酬谢妈祖的保佑。郑和在京师南京、太仓、长乐、湄洲屿等地督造妈祖宫、天妃庙，多次维修各地的妈祖庙宇，并立碑记事，赞颂妈祖护航的功德。郑和在福建长乐县撰立的《天妃灵应之记碑》碑文说："我之云帆高张，昼夜星驰，涉波狂澜，若履通衢者，诚荷朝廷威福之致，尤赖天妃之神护佑之德也。"

从宋代初年始于福建沿海地区的妈祖崇拜，经由明初郑和下西洋的促进和弘扬，得到了更大的发展。其后随着闽粤华人的"下南洋"，妈祖崇拜传播到东南亚，并进而传播到欧美。妈祖文化已发展成为中外炎黄子孙广泛信仰的一种中华民俗文化。

制度文化的交流

西方殖民主义东侵以前，世界东方存在着一个以中国封建王朝为中心的"天朝礼治体系"。郑和七下西洋，忠实地执行永乐皇帝"维护天朝礼治体系"的旨意，遍访亚非30多个国家和地区，通过和平外交，以德服人，以理感人，努力建立以明代中国主导的"天朝礼治体系"，缔造出"梯航万国悉来庭"的旷

that was described as "lots of people from different countries all flocking to flourishing China." Zheng He admirably fulfilled the commission entrusted by Emperor Yongle. Under that historical background, the courtesy system was the supreme system of international relations available in Asia and Africa. It basically featured peace and friendliness as a sort of feudal international order.

Awarding official costumes. While announcing the "imperial edicts" to the Asian and African countries, Zheng He was also entrusted to award them palace costumes of the Ming Dynasty. The costume system was part of the nation's political system. The costumes that Zheng took to those countries included leather hats, crowns, robes, clothes and jade belts for kings, as well as court dresses and ceremonial dresses for general envoys. That helped overseas Asian and African nations copy the official costume system of the Ming Dynasty. In 1409, when he arrived in Malacca, Zheng He read the edicts from Emperor Yongle, conferring the title of king on its chieftain, helping found the kingdom of Malacca and awarding the royal family imperial costumes. Then, the kingdom of Malacca followed the Chinese rituals and courtesy. In addition, there were many other cases where some Asian and African countries requested costumes from the Chinese government of the Ming Dynasty. In 1406, when leaving from China, Sheng Alie Bocheng, the

永乐皇帝在北京皇宫接见满剌加国王率领的外交使团
Emperor Yongle met with the diplomatic mission led by king of Malacca at the imperial palace in Beijing.

世盛景。郑和出色地完成了永乐皇帝交付的在亚非地区建立和维护"天朝礼治体系"的任务。在当时的历史条件下，"天朝礼治体系"是亚非地区所能提供的最高层次的国际关系体系。这种封建的国际秩序，从基本方面讲，是和平的、友好的。

颁赐冠服。郑和下西洋，奉命向亚非国家"颁诏"的同时，还赏赐明朝宫廷的冠服。冠服制度是一个国家政治制度的一部分。郑和颁赐给亚非国家的冠服，给国王的是皮弁、王圭、麟袍、龙衣、犀带、玉

envoy of Borneo, begged Emperor Yongle to award him an imperial belt, a request the emperor satisfied. Many other envoys followed suit, because it really was a great honor for overseas envoys to return imperial belts. The costume system of the Ming Dynasty still has an effect on some Asian and African countries to this day. For instance, the displays in the Thai Palace and the ceremonies held for the king's inspection tours are all from ancient China of the Ming Dynasty. The statues in many of the Thai temples are wearing clothes featuring traditional Ming Dynasty styles and the buttons weaved with fabric strips,

南京勃泥国王墓。1408年，勃泥国王麻那惹加那乃率150多人的使团来中国访问，永乐皇帝以极其隆重的礼仪接待了他们。勃泥国王在南京游览月余，期间不幸染病，虽经御医精心调治，终因病情过重，病逝于南京。永乐皇帝按照王礼埋葬了这位异邦国王。
Bruneian King's Tomb in Nanjing. In 1408, Abdul Majid Hassan, kind of Bruneian, led a delegation of over 150 persons to visit China. Emperor Yongle receipted them with solemn ceremony. The kind of Bruneian visited Nanjing for a month, during which he was suffered from serious disease. Although he accepted careful treatment of the doctors of emperor, he was died in Nanjing. Emperor buried the foreign king in accordance with the ceremony of royal family.

带；赐给一般使节的是朝服、公服。这就将明代中国的官制及其服饰制度"复制"到海外亚非国家。1409年，郑和到满剌加，宣读永乐皇帝敕书，册封其酋长为国王，成立满剌加国，并赐国王、王妃、王子、官吏以仪仗、冠服。于是，该国遂行中国礼仪。除明朝政府主动颁赐冠服以外，也有很多亚非国家请求颁赐中国冠服。1406年，渤泥国使臣生阿烈伯成访问明朝回国前，请求永乐皇帝说："远在海外之人，仰慕中国衣冠礼仪，请授冠带还国。"永乐皇帝满足了他的请求。当时对海外国家使者来说，如能"冠带还国"，是一件令人羡慕的荣耀的事，所以请求者不少。明代中国的冠服制度，至今还可在一些亚非国家中看到它的影响。现在泰国王宫里的陈设以及陈列的泰王出巡仪式，都是中国明朝的式样；泰国很多寺庙里的人物塑像，所穿服饰系中国明朝服饰；胸前用布带编成的纽扣，俗称合桃纽，也是中国明时的旧制。许多亚非国家的使臣到中国访问时主动要求颁赐中国冠服，显示了亚非国家对明代中国先进的文物典章制度的向往。

颁赐历法。历法是国家文明的一项重要标志。郑

also called "peach buttons," are typical of the costumes from the Ming Dynasty. The active requests from envoys of Asian and African nations for Chinese costumes reflected their desire for China's advanced ritual system during the Ming Dynasty.

Awarding Chinese calendars. Calendars are among the major symbols of a nation's civilization. Zheng He was entrusted to give the countries he visited the "Imperial Calendars" and "Chinese Lunar Calendars," both of which noted major events (the former included 30 events and the latter 32). The contents covered a wide range of items from national politics and social life to agricultural production and feudal etiquette, offering the auspicious days for granting awards, offering official posts, dispatching troops, sending envoys, going to school, leaving for trips, opening businesses, doing transactions, sowing seeds, raising animals, offering sacrifice, launching wedding or burial ceremonies and building houses. Following the Chinese calendars, people in Asia and Africa countries were able to better arrange their production and lives, which consequently improved the degree of civilization. For example, people in Champa previously had no knowledge of calendars, taking the phases of the moon as a month, ten months as a year and ten "gengs" ("geng" was a way to measure the time by beating the drums) as a night. They wouldn't sleep until

和奉命向所访亚非国家颁赐《王历》和《农历》。两种历法都有历注，《王历》历注30事，《农历》历注32事，其内容包括国家政治、社会生活、农业生产、封建礼俗等方面，诸如封赏、拜官、出师、遣使、入学、出行、开市、交易、栽种、牧养、祭祀、嫁娶、动土安葬、动工上梁等等。亚非国家有了中国历法，即可遵循仿效，据以安排生产和生活，提高了社会文明程度。举一例以明之。占城国本不懂历法，仅以月亮的圆缺一次作为一个月，十个月为一年，敲鼓十更为一夜，人们每天不到子时（夜里11点到1点）不睡觉，不到午时（白天11点到1点）不起床。每当月亮升起，就喝酒跳舞作乐。郑和去后颁赐中国历法，该国才知有闰月和24节气的划分；改夜鼓为八更，这对该国天文气象的发展和人民生产、生活的科学安排，起到了促进作用。

输出中国铜钱。郑和出使，每次都携带大量的中国铜钱，或作馈赠之用，或作贸易之用。郑和船队通过赏赐、贸易等方式输出的中国铜钱，大量传播到东南亚，致使原来使用贝币的东南亚国家过渡到使用中国钱币。奉行中国货币制度，大大有利于东南亚的商

"Zishi" (from 11:00 p.m. to 1:00 a.m.) and wouldn't get up till "Wushi" (from 11:00 a.m. to 1:00 p.m.), and they went to drink and dance every night when the moon rose. With the calendars Zheng He gave away, local people learnt about the divisions of the 24 solar terms and intercalary months. They also reduced the nighttime to eight drum beats. These changes greatly pushed the development of astronomy and meteorology and gave people a more scientific agenda for their lives and production.

Exporting Chinese copper coins. Zheng He would carry lots of Chinese copper coins during his visits to give away or trade. The Chinese copper coins Zheng He's fleet exported soon spread across Southeast Asia and this led to the replacement of shells by Chinese copper coins in those countries. Good for the circulation of commodities, the Chinese currency system was used from the 15th century to the eve of World War II in the 20th century. Today, the inhabitants in Bali, Indonesia, still use strings of Chinese copper coins as indispensable divine instruments in religious ceremonies.

"Zheng He made prominent contributions in developing trade in Southeast Asia and improving people's lives. Chinese copper coins, meteorology system and governmental organizations that were widely trusted across Southeast Asia were all introduced by Zheng He during his voyages," said Zhao Zehong, a contemporary

肯尼亚的拉姆岛自古就是中国商品在东非的集散地，被称为"中国的拉姆"。
The Lamu Island in Kenya has been the distribution place of Chinese commodities in East Africa since the ancient time, and was thus called "Lamu of China"

品流通。中国的货币金融制度自15世纪起通行了几个世纪，直到20世纪第二次世界大战前才停止。现在印尼巴厘岛一带的居民，又将中国铜钱结成一串一串吊起来，作为宗教仪式上不可或缺的神器使用。

当代马来西亚学者赵泽洪说："在发展南洋经济贸易、改善生活方面，郑和作出了突出的贡献。南洋各国各地都信任的中国钱币、度量衡制度和政府组织等等，都是郑和下西洋期间从中国带出来而在南洋流通、通行的。"

敷宣文教。郑和使团在海外直接或间接帮助亚非

Malaysian scholar.

Advocating Chinese culture and religion. While going out to help other countries establish their own systems of politics, rituals, laws and currencies, Zheng's fleet also invited foreign envoys to visit China, with a view to better imparting on them Chinese culture and rituals. For example, during traditional festivals, foreign envoys would be invited to mingle with Chinese people, attending dinner parties, shootings and lantern shows and visiting parks or gardens. In 1423, over 1,200 envoys from 16 Asian and African countries including Hormuz in West Asia returned with Zheng He to China for a visit. They were further invited to the grand ceremony of "entering Juyongguan" launched by Emperor Yongle two months later. Naturally, it's no wonder the envoys, who saw all the grandness of the Chinese rituals and etiquettes in person, were deeply attracted by Chinese civilization and morality and urgently hoped for a change in their backward conventions.

Zheng's voyages to the Western Oceans increased the material, spiritual and institutional cultural exchanges between China and the rest of Asia and Africa, and greatly pushed forward the social and economic development of the Asian and African countries, Southeast Asian countries in particular. This is why the people in Southeast Asia regard Zheng He as the man from the gods

国家建立健全国家制度、礼仪制度、法律制度、货币制度，邀请各国使节到中国访问，使其目睹中国的社会文明，接受中华礼仪的熏陶。逢喜庆节会，明廷常邀外国使节与臣民同乐，参加酒宴、射击、观灯、游园等活动。1423年郑和第六次下西洋时，曾偕同包括西亚忽鲁谟斯在内的亚非16个国家的1200余名使臣随郑和船队访问明朝。16国使臣在中国访问两个月后，又应邀参加迎接永乐皇帝"车入居庸关"的盛典。1200名外国使臣亲身感受明朝政府和中国人民的优厚礼遇，亲见中国文物典章之美，目睹"天朝太平乐事之盛"，自然为中华文教道德的魅力所吸引，仰慕中华文明制度，愿意改变自己欠文明的落后习俗。

郑和下西洋促进了中国与亚非国家之间的物质文化、精神文化和制度文化的交流，大大推进了亚非国家尤其是东南亚国家社会经济文化的发展。正因为如此，东南亚各国人民把郑和视为上帝的福荫，把郑和奉为神灵，顶礼膜拜直到今天。东南亚人民视野中的郑和，历经600多年文化积淀，已然衍变成具有多方文化内涵和象征意义的符号，进而从明代中国的历史文化范畴演化为具有本区域历史内涵的文化现象。从这

whom they have honored and adored to this day. In their eyes, the name of "Zheng He" has become a symbol that incorporates diverse cultural connotations after 600-plus years of evolution.

At the same time, the Chinese historical episode from the Ming Dynasty has grown into a cultural phenomenon with local historical connotations. In this sense, Zheng He was significant to more than just Chinese history; he was a giant respected by all people across Southeast Asia and even the world. The history of Zheng He's voyages boosted Sino-foreign cultural exchanges and demonstrates that culture has no walls or boundaries. It is the common wealth created by all humans. Culture flows from higher locations to lower ones and from places where it is abundant to places where it is wanted. There is no exception to this in modern or ancient times in China or elsewhere. Exporting culture shall be deemed as an obligation of culturally advanced countries, rather than a favor. Importing an alien culture is a right, not a shameful weakness. Cultural exchanges are needed around the world. They help human culture and society advance. Nobody can stop their positive effects upon human history.

During the Sino-foreign cultural exchanges triggered by Zheng's voyages, the Chinese culture of the Ming Dynasty contributed its treasures to Asian and African

肯尼亚帕泰岛上自称祖先来自中国的法茂人。据肯尼亚博物馆的介绍，曾经有一艘郑和船队的船只在帕泰岛附近触礁，船上约400人登上该岛。当地首长准许他们定居，并准其与当地女子通婚。他们的后代称为"法茂人"。

People in the Pate Island in Kenya claimed that their ancestors are Famao people from China. According to the introduction of Kenya Museum, a ship from Zheng He's fleet hit on the rocks near the Pate Island. Over 400 persons in the ship stepped on the island. The local headman allowed them to live permanently and to marry with local girls. They were called Famao people by the descendants.

个意义来说，郑和不仅是中华民族的历史伟人，也是东南亚乃至全世界人民共同敬仰的历史伟人。

郑和下西洋推动中外文化交流的史实说明：文化没有围墙，文化没有国界。它是人类创造的共同财富。文化是流动的，从高处到低处、从充实的地方到空虚的地方流动，古今中外毫无不同。输出文化到异国，应当看作是先进国家的责任，而不可看作恩惠；接受异国先进文化，应当看作是一种权利，而不应讳为缺点。文化交流是人类的需要。它促进了人类文化的发展，推动着人类社会前进。文化交流一旦进行，其碰撞交融后所激发出来的历史进步作用是任何人都无法阻止的。在郑和下西洋引发的中外文化交流中，明代中国文化向亚非国家贡献了自己的珍品，同时也吸纳亚非国家文

nations and, at the same time, absorbed the essence of the alien cultures and grew more diversified. There were quite a few sailors in Zheng's fleet who couldn't continue the trips because of hurricanes, robberies or diseases. For survival, they had to stay on overseas islands, where they worked hard and raised offspring. They became the first group of overseas Chinese in those places. Zheng He's voyages made the sea routes between China and the countries in the Western Oceans completely smooth. Furthermore, the advanced Chinese culture Zheng He's fleet exported to Southeast Asia laid a foundation for the region to flourish. Both paved way for the mass migration to Southeast Asia by Chinese people, especially those in China's southeast Fujian and Guangdong provinces. The historical facts prove that overseas Chinese were the main force in the social development of Southeast Asia. In this regard, it can be said that Zheng He's voyages to the Western Oceans kicked off mass Chinese migration to Southeast Asia and the later development.

化的精华，丰富提高了自身。

　　郑和船队船员在航海过程中，或遭风漂泊，或遇寇被掠，或病虐不能续航者，为数不少。这些人员留居海外岛屿，为了生存，必然努力开发荒岛，并传育子孙，成为这些岛屿上最早的一批华侨。郑和下西洋完全打通了中国通往西洋各国的海上通道，加之郑和船队向南洋人民传输中国先进文化，使南洋地区显示出广阔的开发前景，这就为更多的中国人特别是东南沿海如闽广两省的人民"下南洋"创造了条件。后来的事实证明：华侨是开发南洋、促进南洋社会发展的生力军。故从这个意义来考量，可以说，郑和下西洋揭开了华侨大量徙居南洋、开发南洋的序幕。

$2000